THE AENEID

Virgil

TECHNICAL DIRECTOR Maxwell Krohn
EDITORIAL DIRECTOR Justin Kestler
MANAGING EDITOR Ben Florman

SERIES EDITORS Boomie Aglietti, Justin Kestler
PRODUCTION Christian Lorentzen

WRITERS Patrick Gardner, Matilda Santos
EDITORS Sarah Friedberg, Christian Lorentzen

This edition published by Spark Publishing

Spark Publishing
A Division of SparkNotes LLC
120 Fifth Avenue, 8th Floor
New York, NY 10011

02 03 04 05 SN 9 8 7 6 5 4 3 2 1

Please send all comments and questions or report errors to
feedback@sparknotes.com.

Library of Congress information available upon request

Printed and bound in the United States

RRD-C

ISBN 1-58663-376-7

Introduction:
Stopping to
Buy SparkNotes
on a
Snowy Evening

Whose words these are you *think* you know.
Your paper's due tomorrow, though;
We're glad to see you stopping here
To get some help before you go.

Lost your course? You'll find it here.
Face tests and essays without fear.
Between the words, good grades at stake:
Get great results throughout the year.

Once school bells caused your heart to quake
As teachers circled each mistake.
Use SparkNotes and no longer weep,
Ace every single test you take.

Yes, books are lovely, dark, and deep,
But only what you grasp you keep,
With hours to go before you sleep,
With hours to go before you sleep.

CONTENTS

NOTE: This SparkNote is based on the Vintage Classics edition of the *Aeneid*, translated by Robert Fitzgerald. All other English translations vary in language and line numbering.

CONTEXT

VIRGIL, THE PREEMINENT POET of the Roman Empire, was born Publius Vergilius Maro on October 15, 70 B.C., near Mantua, a city in northern Italy. The son of a farmer, Virgil studied in Cremona, then in Milan, and finally in Rome. Around 41 B.C., he returned to Mantua to begin work on his *Eclogues*, which he published in 37 B.C. Soon afterward, civil war forced him to flee south to Naples, where seven years later he finished his second work, the *Georgics*, a long poem on farming. Virgil's writing gained him the recognition of the public, wealth from patrons, and the favor of the emperor.

Virgil lived at the height of the first age of the Roman Empire, during the reign of the emperor Octavian, later known as Augustus. Before Augustus became emperor, though, internal strife plagued the Roman government. During Virgil's youth, the First Triumvirate—Julius Caesar, Pompey, and Crassus—governed the Roman Republic. Crassus was killed around 53 B.C., and Caesar initiated civil war against Pompey. After defeating Pompey, Caesar reigned alone until the Ides of March in 44 B.C., when Brutus and Cassius, two senators, assassinated him. Civil war erupted between the assassins and the Second Triumvirate—Octavian, Antony, and Lepidus. By 36 B.C. only Octavian and Antony remained, and they began warring against each other. At the Battle of Actium in 31 B.C., Octavian defeated Antony and his ally Cleopatra of Egypt, finally consolidating power in himself alone. Four years later, he assumed the title Augustus. Virgil witnessed all this turmoil, and the warring often disrupted his life.

Immediately after finishing the *Georgics*, Virgil began his masterwork, the *Aeneid*. He was fortunate enough to enter the good graces of Augustus, and, in part, the *Aeneid* serves to legitimize Augustus's reign. The *Aeneid* tells the story of the Trojan hero Aeneas's perilous flight from Troy to Italy following the Trojan War. In Italy, Aeneas's descendents would go on to found Rome. In the epic, Virgil repeatedly foreshadows the coming of Augustus, perhaps to silence critics who claimed that he achieved power through violence and treachery. (Whether or not Virgil truly believed all the praise he heaped upon Augustus is a matter of debate.) When Rome was at its height, the easiest way to justify the recent brutal events was to claim that the civil wars and the changes in leadership had been decreed by fate to usher in the reign of the great Augustus. Yet the *Aeneid* is by no means a purely political work; like other epic poems, its subject stands on its own as a story for all time.

Virgil did not invent the story that Rome descended from Troy; he crafted the events narrated in the *Aeneid* from an existing tradition surrounding Aeneas that extended from the ancient Greek poet Homer through the contemporary Roman historian Livy. In Book XX of the *Iliad,* Aeneas faces off with Achilles, and we learn about Aeneas's lineage and his reputation for bravery. However, in that scene, he is no match for Achilles, who has been outfitted in armor forged by the divine smith Hephaestus. Poseidon rescues Aeneas from certain doom and praises the Trojan for his piety. Poseidon also prophesies that Aeneas will survive the Trojan War and assume leadership over the Trojan people.

Ancient accounts of Aeneas's postwar wanderings vary. Greek art from the sixth century B.C. portrays Aeneas carrying his father, Anchises, out from the burning ruins of Troy. Archaeological evidence suggests that the myth of Aeneas was often depicted in art on the Italian mainland as early as the sixth century B.C. The settlement of Aeneas and the Trojans in Italy and their connection with the foundation of Rome entered the written tradition centuries after Homer, at the end of the third century B.C. Earlier poets, including the Roman Varro, had connected Dido and Aeneas, but Virgil was the first to tie all the elements of Aeneas's story together in epic form.

After eleven years of composition, the meticulous Virgil did not consider the *Aeneid* fit for publication. He planned to spend three years editing it, but fell ill returning from a trip to Greece. Just before his death on September 21, 19 B.C., he ordered the manuscript of the *Aeneid* to be burned, because he still considered it unfinished. Augustus intervened, however, arranging for the poem to be published against Virgil's wishes.

Virgil's masterful and meticulously crafted poetry earned him a legacy as the greatest poet in the Latin language. Throughout the Middle Ages and into the Renaissance, his fame only grew. Before the invention of the printing press, when classical texts, transmitted by the hands of scribes, were scarce, Virgil's poetry was available to the literate classes, among whom he was regarded as the most significant writer of antiquity. He inspired poets across languages, including Dante in Italian, Milton in English, and an anonymous

French poet who reworked the *Aeneid* into the medieval romance *Le Roman d'Eneas*. In what became a Christian culture, Virgil was viewed as a pagan prophet because several lines in his works were interpreted as predictions of the coming of Christ. Among writers of the Renaissance, Virgil was appreciated for the fluidity of his rigorously structured poetry and his vivid portrayals of human emotion.

Modern critics, on the other hand, have been less kind. Virgil's poetry is often judged in relation to that of his Greek predecessors, especially the *Iliad* and the *Odyssey,* epics attributed to Homer that also portray the Trojan War and its aftermath. Most contemporary scholars hold that Virgil's poetry pales in comparison to Homer's. Virgil himself often viewed his poetry in light of Homer's; he invoked such comparisons within the *Aeneid* and wished to surpass the Greek poet, while still borrowing from him heavily. Virgil's poetry does not possess the same originality of expression as Homeric epic poetry. The *Aeneid* shares with the *Iliad* and the *Odyssey* a tone of ironic tragedy, as characters act against their own wishes, submit their lives to fate, and often meet dark ends. Most scholars agree that Virgil distinguished himself within the epic tradition of antiquity by representing the broad spectrum of human emotion in his characters as they are subsumed in the historical tides of dislocation and war.

PLOT OVERVIEW

ON THE MEDITERRANEAN SEA, Aeneas and his fellow Trojans flee from their home city of Troy, which has been destroyed by the Greeks. They sail for Italy, where Aeneas is destined to found Rome. As they near their destination, a fierce storm throws them off course and lands them in Carthage. Dido, Carthage's founder and queen, welcomes them. Aeneas relates to Dido the long and painful story of his group's travels thus far.

Aeneas tells of the sack of Troy that ended the Trojan War after ten years of Greek siege. In the final campaign, the Trojans were tricked when they accepted into their city walls a wooden horse that, unbeknownst to them, harbored several Greek soldiers in its hollow belly. He tells how he escaped the burning city with his father, Anchises, his son, Ascanius, and the hearth gods that represent their fallen city. Assured by the gods that a glorious future awaited him in Italy, he set sail with a fleet containing the surviving citizens of Troy. Aeneas relates the ordeals they faced on their journey. Twice they attempted to build a new city, only to be driven away by bad omens and plagues. Harpies, creatures that are part woman and part bird, cursed them, but they also encountered friendly countrymen unexpectedly. Finally, after the loss of Anchises and a bout of terrible weather, they made their way to Carthage.

Impressed by Aeneas's exploits and sympathetic to his suffering, Dido, a Phoenician princess who fled her home and founded Carthage after her brother murdered her husband, falls in love with Aeneas. They live together as lovers for a period, until the gods remind Aeneas of his duty to found a new city. He determines to set sail once again. Dido is devastated by his departure, and kills herself by ordering a huge pyre to be built with Aeneas's castaway possessions, climbing upon it, and stabbing herself with the sword Aeneas leaves behind.

As the Trojans make for Italy, bad weather blows them to Sicily, where they hold funeral games for the dead Anchises. The women, tired of the voyage, begin to burn the ships, but a downpour puts the fires out. Some of the travel-weary stay behind, while Aeneas, reinvigorated after his father visits him in a dream, takes the rest on toward Italy. Once there, Aeneas descends into the underworld, guided by the Sibyl of Cumae, to visit his father. He is shown a pageant of the future history and heroes of Rome, which helps him to understand the importance of his mission. Aeneas returns from the underworld, and the Trojans continue up the coast to the region of Latium.

The arrival of the Trojans in Italy begins peacefully. King Latinus, the Italian ruler, extends his hospitality, hoping that Aeneas will prove to be the foreigner whom, according to a prophecy, his daughter Lavinia is supposed to marry. But Latinus's wife, Amata, has other ideas. She means for Lavinia to marry Turnus, a local suitor. Amata and Turnus cultivate enmity toward the newly arrived Trojans. Meanwhile, Ascanius hunts a stag that was a pet of the local herdsmen. A fight breaks out, and several people are killed. Turnus, riding this current of anger, begins a war.

Aeneas, at the suggestion of the river god Tiberinus, sails north up the Tiber to seek military support among the neighboring tribes. During this voyage, his mother, Venus, descends to give him a new set of weapons, wrought by Vulcan. While the Trojan leader is away, Turnus attacks. Aeneas returns to find his countrymen embroiled in battle. Pallas, the son of Aeneas's new ally Evander, is killed by Turnus. Aeneas flies into a violent fury, and many more are slain by the day's end.

The two sides agree to a truce so that they can bury the dead, and the Latin leaders discuss whether to continue the battle. They decide to spare any further unnecessary carnage by proposing a hand-to-hand duel between Aeneas and Turnus. When the two leaders face off, however, the other men begin to quarrel, and full-scale battle resumes. Aeneas is wounded in the thigh, but eventually the Trojans threaten the enemy city. Turnus rushes out to meet Aeneas, who wounds Turnus badly. Aeneas nearly spares Turnus but, remembering the slain Pallas, slays him instead.

Character List

Mortals

Aeneas   The protagonist of the *Aeneid*. Aeneas is a survivor of the siege of Troy, a city on the coast of Asia Minor. His defining characteristic is piety, a respect for the will of the gods. He is a fearsome warrior and a leader able to motivate his men in the face of adversity, but also a man capable of great compassion and sorrow. His destiny is to found the Roman race in Italy and he subordinates all other concerns to this mission. The *Aeneid* is about his journey from Troy to Italy, which enables him to fulfill his fate.

Dido   The queen of Carthage, a city in northern Africa, in what is now Libya, and lover of Aeneas. Dido left the land of Tyre when her husband was murdered by Pygmalion, her brother. She and her city are strong, but she becomes an unfortunate pawn of the gods in their struggle for Aeneas's destiny. Her love for Aeneas, provoked by Venus, proves to be her downfall. After he abandons her, she constructs a funeral pyre and stabs herself upon it with Aeneas's sword.

Turnus   The ruler of the Rutulians in Italy. Turnus is Aeneas's major antagonist among mortals. He is Lavinia's leading suitor until Aeneas arrives. This rivalry incites him to wage war against the Trojans, despite Latinus's willingness to allow the Trojans to settle in Latium and Turnus's understanding that he cannot successfully defy fate. He is brash and fearless, a capable soldier who values his honor over his life.

Ascanius   Aeneas's young son by his first wife, Creusa. Ascanius (also called Iulus) is most important as a symbol of Aeneas's destiny—his future founding of the Roman race. Though still a child, Ascanius has several opportunities over the course of the epic to display his bravery and leadership. He leads a procession of boys on horseback during the games of Book V and he helps to defend the Trojan camp from Turnus's attack while his father is away.

Anchises   Aeneas's father, and a symbol of Aeneas's Trojan heritage. Although Anchises dies during the journey from Troy to Italy, he continues in spirit to help his son fulfill fate's decrees, especially by guiding Aeneas through the underworld and showing him what fate has in store for his descendants.

Creusa   Aeneas's wife at Troy, and the mother of Ascanius. Creusa is lost and killed as her family attempts to flee the city, but tells Aeneas he will find a new wife at his new home.

Sinon   The Greek youth who pretends to have been left behind at the end of the Trojan War. Sinon persuades the Trojans to take in the wooden horse as an offering to Minerva, then lets out the warriors trapped inside the horse's belly.

Latinus   The king of the Latins, the people of what is now central Italy, around the Tiber River. Latinus allows Aeneas into his kingdom and encourages him to become a suitor of Lavinia, his daughter, causing resentment and eventually war among his subjects. He respects the gods and fate, but does not hold strict command over his people.

Lavinia   Latinus's daughter and a symbol of Latium in general. Lavinia's character is not developed in the poem; she is important only as the object of the Trojan-Latin struggle. The question of who will marry Lavinia—Turnus or Aeneas—becomes key to future relations between the Latins and the Trojans and therefore the *Aeneid's* entire historical scheme.

Amata	Queen of Laurentum (a region of Latium, in Italy) and wife of Latinus. Amata opposes the marriage of Lavinia, her daughter, to Aeneas and remains loyal throughout to Turnus, Lavinia's original suitor. Amata kills herself once it is clear that Aeneas is destined to win.
Evander	King of Pallanteum (a region of Arcadia, in Italy) and father of Pallas. Evander is a sworn enemy of the Latins, and Aeneas befriends him and secures his assistance in the battles against Turnus.
Pallas	Son of Evander, whom Evander entrusts to Aeneas's care and tutelage. Pallas eventually dies in battle at the hands of Turnus, causing Aeneas and Evander great grief. To avenge Pallas's death, Aeneas finally slays Turnus, dismissing an initial impulse to spare him.
Drancës	A Latin leader who desires an end to the Trojan-Latin struggle. Drancës questions the validity of Turnus's motives at the council of the Latins, infuriating Turnus.
Camilla	The leader of the Volscians, a race of warrior maidens. Camilla is perhaps the only strong mortal female character in the epic.
Juturna	Turnus's sister. Juno provokes Juturna into inducing a full-scale battle between the Latins and the Trojans by disguising herself as an officer and goading the Latins after a treaty has already been reached.
Achates	A Trojan and a personal friend of Aeneas.

GODS AND GODDESSES

Juno	The queen of the gods, the wife and sister of Jupiter, and the daughter of Saturn. Juno (Hera in Greek mythology) hates the Trojans because of the Trojan Paris's judgment against her in a beauty contest. She is

also a patron of Carthage and knows that Aeneas's Roman descendants are destined to destroy Carthage. She takes out her anger on Aeneas throughout the epic, and in her wrath acts as his primary divine antagonist.

Venus   The goddess of love and the mother of Aeneas. Venus (Aphrodite in Greek mythology) is a benefactor of the Trojans. She helps her son whenever Juno tries to hurt him, causing conflict among the gods. She is also referred to as Cytherea, after Cythera, the island where she was born and where her shrine is located.

Jupiter   The king of the gods, and the son of Saturn. While the gods often struggle against one another in battles of will, Jupiter's will reigns supreme and becomes identified with the more impersonal force of fate. Therefore, Jupiter (also known as Jove, and called Zeus in Greek mythology) directs the general progress of Aeneas's destiny, ensuring that Aeneas is never permanently thrown off his course toward Italy. Jupiter's demeanor is controlled and levelheaded compared to the volatility of Juno and Venus.

Neptune   God of the sea, and generally an ally of Venus and Aeneas. Neptune (Poseidon in Greek mythology) calms the storm that opens the epic and conducts Aeneas safely on the last leg of his voyage.

Mercury   The messenger god. The other gods often send Mercury (Hermes in Greek mythology) on errands to Aeneas.

Aeolus   The god of the winds, enlisted to aid Juno in creating bad weather for the Trojans in Book I.

Cupid   A son of Venus and the god of erotic desire. In Book I, Cupid (Eros in Greek mythology) disguises himself as Ascanius, Aeneas's son, and causes Dido to fall in love with Aeneas.

Allecto One of the Furies, or deities who avenge sins, sent by Juno in Book IV to incite the Latin people to war against the Trojans.

Vulcan God of fire and the forge, and husband of Venus. Venus urges Vulcan (Hephaestus in Greek mythology) to craft a superior set of arms for Aeneas, and the gift serves Aeneas well in his battle with Turnus.

Tiberinus The river god associated with the Tiber River, where Rome will eventually be built. At Tiberinus's suggestion, Aeneas travels upriver to make allies of the Arcadians.

Saturn The father of the gods. Saturn (Chronos in Greek mythology) was king of Olympus until his son Jupiter overthrew him.

Minerva The goddess who protects the Greeks during the Trojan War and helps them conquer Troy. Like Juno, Minerva (Pallas Athena in Greek mythology) is motivated against the Trojans by the Trojan Paris's judgment that Venus was the most beautiful among goddesses.

Apollo A son of Jupiter and god of the sun. Apollo was born at Delos and helps the Trojans in their voyage when they stop there. Because he is often portrayed as an archer, many characters invoke his name before they fire a shaft in battle.

CHARACTERS FROM HOMER'S *ILIAD* RELEVANT TO THE *AENEID*

Ulysses The hero of Homer's *Odyssey,* and one of the captains of the Greek army that takes Troy. Ulysses (Odysseus in Greek lore), like Aeneas, must make a long and treacherous voyage before he finds home again, and references to his whereabouts in the *Aeneid* help situate Aeneas's wanderings in relation to Ulysses'.

Achilles   The greatest of the Greek warriors. Achilles slew the Trojan hero Hector during the war and is the tragic hero of the *Iliad*.

Hector   The greatest of the Trojan warriors, killed at Troy. Hector is in some ways a parallel figure to Turnus, who also defends his native city to the death.

Andromachë Hector's wife, who survives the siege of Troy. Andromachë meets Aeneas in his wanderings, tells him her story, and advises his course to Italy.

Paris   A Trojan prince, son of Priam and Hecuba, and brother of Hector. The handsomest of men, Paris is asked to judge which goddess is most beautiful: Venus, Juno, or Minerva. Venus promises him Helen as his wife in exchange for his judgment, so Paris selects Venus. This selection inspires the permanent wrath of Juno against the Trojans. Stealing Helen from her Greek husband, Menelaus, Paris provokes the Trojan War.

Helen   The most beautiful of mortal women and wife of Menelaus. Helen's abduction to Troy by Paris sparks the Trojan War.

Menelaus A Greek king who wed Helen and made a pact with her other suitors to fight anyone who tried to steal her. When Paris took Helen, the pact was invoked and the Trojan War began.

Agamemnon The leader of the Greek army at Troy, and the king of Argos, a city in Greece. Upon his return from the war, Agamemnon is killed by his adulterous wife, Clytemnestra.

Priam   The king of Troy. Priam is slain before Aeneas's eyes during the Greeks' sacking of Troy.

Pyrrhus   The son of Achilles. Pyrrhus, also called Neoptolemus, appears in Aeneas's account of the siege of Troy as the brutal murderer of Priam and Priam's sons.

CHARACTER LIST

ANALYSIS OF MAJOR CHARACTERS

AENEAS

As the son of the Trojan mortal Anchises and Venus, the goddess of beauty and erotic love, Aeneas enjoys a special divine protection. He is chosen to survive the siege of Troy and to lay the foundations in Italy for the glory of the Roman Empire. In the *Aeneid*, Aeneas's fate as Rome's founder drives all the action, and the narrative constantly points out that Aeneas's heroism owes as much to his legacy as to his own actions. Aeneas serves as the vehicle through which fate carries out its historical design.

As a Trojan leader, Aeneas respects prophecy and attempts to incorporate the idea of his own destiny into his actions, in spite of emotional impulses that conflict with his fated duties. His ability to accept his destined path despite his unhappiness in doing so makes him a graceful hero and a worthy recipient of the honor and favor the gods bestow upon him. His compassion for the sufferings of others, even in conjunction with a single-minded devotion to his duty, is another aspect of his heroism. Sympathetic to the weariness of others on the journey, he delivers speeches to his fleet to keep the men's spirits high.

Aeneas's personal investment in the future of Rome increases as the story progresses. The events of Book V, in which the Trojans sail away from Carthage toward Italy, and Book VI, in which Aeneas visits his father in the realm of the dead, depict Aeneas's growth as a leader. In Book V, he shows his sympathy for the woes of others by allowing the crippled and unwilling to stay behind. He also grows in compassion in the underworld when he observes the lot of the unburied dead. He carries these lessons into the war that follows, taking care to ensure the proper burial of both ally and enemy.

When, in the underworld, Aeneas's father, Anchises, presents a tableau of the events that will lead to Rome's pinnacle, Aeneas comes to understand his historical role with greater clarity and immediacy. The scenes depicted later in the epic on the shield made by Vulcan further focus Aeneas's sentiments and actions toward his destined future. There are moments, of course, when Aeneas seems to lose track of his destiny—particularly during his dalliance with Dido in Carthage. Aeneas is recalled to his duty in this case not by a long historical vision, but by an appeal from Jupiter to his obligation to his son, Ascanius, to whom Aeneas is devoted.

Even prior to Virgil's treatment of the Trojan War, Aeneas held a place in the classical tradition as a figure of great piety, just as Ulysses was known for his cunning and Achilles for his rage in battle. The value Aeneas places on family is particularly evident in the scene in which he escorts his father and son out of Troy, bearing his elderly father on his back. He behaves no less honorably toward the gods, earnestly seeking to find out their wishes and conform to them as fully as possible. His words to Dido in Books IV and VI express his commitment to obey fate rather than indulge his feelings of genuine romantic love. This subordination of personal desire to duty defines Aeneas's character and earns him the repeated moniker "pious Aeneas." His behavior contrasts with Juno's and Turnus's in this regard, as those characters both fight fate every step of the way.

DIDO

Before Aeneas's arrival, Dido is the confident and competent ruler of Carthage, a city she founded on the coast of North Africa. She is resolute, we learn, in her determination not to marry again and to preserve the memory of her dead husband, Sychaeus, whose murder at the hands of Pygmalion, her brother, caused her to flee her native Tyre. Despite this turmoil, she maintains her focus on her political responsibilities.

Virgil depicts the suddenness of the change that love provokes in the queen with the image of Dido as the victim of Cupid's arrow, which strikes her almost like madness or a disease. Dido tells her sister that a flame has been reignited within her. While flames and fire are traditional, almost clichéd images associated with love, fire is also a natural force of destruction and uncontrollable chaos. Dido risks everything by falling for Aeneas, and when this love fails, she finds herself unable to reassume her dignified position. By taking Aeneas as a lover, she compromises her previously untainted loyalty to her dead husband's memory. She loses the support of Carthage's citizens, who have seen their queen indulge an amorous obsession at the expense of her civic responsibilities. Further, by dallying with another foreigner, Dido alienates the local African chieftains who had approached her as suitors and now pose a military threat. Her irrational obsession drives her to a frenzied suicide, out of the tragedy of her situation and the pain of lost love, but also out of a sense of diminished possibilities for the future.

Dido plays a role in the first four books of the epic similar to that which Turnus plays at the end. She is a figure of passion and volatility, qualities that contrast with Aeneas's order and control, and traits that Virgil associated with Rome itself in his own day. Dido also represents the sacrifice Aeneas makes to pursue his duty. If fate were to allow him to remain in Carthage, he would rule a city beside a queen he loves without enduring the further hardships of war. Aeneas encounters Dido's shade in the underworld just before the future legacy of Rome is revealed to him, and again he admits that his abandonment of the queen was not an act of his own will. This encounter with lost love, though poignant, is dwarfed by Anchises' subsequent revelation of the glory of Rome. Through Dido, Virgil affirms order, duty, and history at the expense of romantic love.

TURNUS

Turnus is a counterpart to Dido, another of Juno's protégés who must eventually perish in order for Aeneas to fulfill his destiny. Both Turnus and Dido represent forces of irrationality in contrast to Aeneas's pious sense of order. Dido is undone by her romantic desire, Turnus by his unrelenting rage and pride. He is famous for courage and skill in battle, and justly so: he has all the elements of a hero.

What distinguishes Turnus from Aeneas, besides his unmitigated fury in battle, is his willfulness. He tries to carve out his own understanding of history with his prediction of his own success, based on the events of the Trojan past, as told in Homer's *Iliad*. Though Turnus may appear to us a Latin version of Achilles, the raging hero of the *Iliad*, Turnus's powers as a warrior are not enough to guarantee him victory. Jupiter has decreed another destiny for Turnus, an outcome Turnus refuses to accept. Turnus's interpretation of signs and omens is similarly stubborn. He interprets them to his own advantage rather than seeking their true meaning, as Aeneas does.

Turnus's character changes in the last few battle scenes, when we see him gradually lose confidence as he comes to understand and accept his tragic fate. He is angry earlier when Juno tries to protect him by luring him out of the battle and onto a ship. In this episode she humiliates him, making him look like a coward rather than the hero he so desperately wants to be. By the final scenes, however, his resistance to the aid of Juturna, his sister, is motivated no longer by a fiery determination to fight but by a quiet resolve to meet his fate and die honorably.

CHARACTER ANALYSIS

THEMES, MOTIFS & SYMBOLS

THEMES

Themes are the fundamental and often universal ideas explored in a literary work.

THE PRIMACY OF FATE
The direction and destination of Aeneas's course are preordained, and his various sufferings and glories in battle and at sea over the course of the epic merely postpone this unchangeable destiny. The power of fate stands above the power of the gods in the hierarchy of supernatural forces. Often it is associated with the will of Jupiter, the most powerful of the Olympians. Because Jupiter's will trumps the wills of all others, the interference in Aeneas's life by the lesser gods, who strive to advance their personal interests as much as they can within the contours of the larger destiny, do not really affect the overall outcome of events.

The development of individual characters in the epic is apparent in the readiness and resistance with which they meet the directives of fate. Juno and Turnus both fight destiny every step of the way, and so the epic's final resolution involves a transformation in each of them, as a result of which they resign themselves to fate and allow the story, at last, to arrive at its destined end. Dido desires Aeneas, whom fate denies her, and her desire consumes her. Aeneas preserves his sanity, as well as his own life and those of his men, by subordinating his own anxieties and desires to the demands of fate and the rules of piety. Fate, to Virgil's Roman audience, is a divine, religious principle that determines the course of history and has culminated in the Roman Empire.

THE SUFFERINGS OF WANDERERS
The first half of the *Aeneid* tells the story of the Trojans' wanderings as they make their way from Troy to Italy. Ancient culture was oriented toward familial loyalty and geographic origin, and stressed the idea that a homeland is one's source of identity. Because homeless-

ness implies instability of both situation and identity, it is a form of suffering in and of itself. But Virgil adds to the sufferings of the wandering Trojans by putting them at the mercy of forces larger than themselves. On the sea, their fleet buffeted by frequent storms, the Trojans must repeatedly decide on a course of action in an uncertain world. The Trojans also feel disoriented each time they land on an unknown shore or learn where they are without knowing whether it is the place where they belong. As an experience that, from the point of view of the Trojans, is uncertain in every way, the long wanderings at sea serve as a metaphor for the kind of wandering that is characteristic of life in general. We and Virgil's Roman audience know what fate has in store for the Trojans, but the wandering characters themselves do not. Because these individual human beings are not always privy to the larger picture of destiny, they are still vulnerable to fears, surprises, desires, and unforeseen triumphs.

THE GLORY OF ROME

Virgil wrote the *Aeneid* during what is known as the Golden Age of the Roman Empire, under the auspices of Rome's first emperor, Caesar Augustus. Virgil's purpose was to write a myth of Rome's origins that would emphasize the grandeur and legitimize the success of an empire that had conquered most of the known world. The *Aeneid* steadily points toward this already realized cultural pinnacle; Aeneas even justifies his settlement in Latium in the same manner that the empire justified its settlement in numerous other foreign territories. Virgil works backward, connecting the political and social situation of his own day with the inherited tradition of the Greek gods and heroes, to show the former as historically derived from the latter. Order and good government triumph emphatically over the Italian peoples, whose world prior to the Trojans' arrival is characterized as a primitive existence of war, chaos, and emotional irrationality. By contrast, the empire under Augustus was generally a world of peace, order, and emotional stability.

MOTIFS

Motifs are recurring structures, contrasts, or literary devices that can help to develop and inform the text's major themes.

PROPHECIES AND PREDICTIONS
Prophecy and prediction take many forms in the *Aeneid*, including dreams, visitations from the dead, mysterious signs and omens, and direct visitations of the gods or their divine messengers. These windows onto the future orient mortal characters toward fate as they try to glean, sometimes clearly and sometimes dimly, what is to come. Virgil's audience, however, hears these predictions with the advantage of hindsight, looking backward to observe the realization of an already accomplished fate. As observers who know about the future, the audience is in the same position as the gods, and the tension between the audience's and the characters' perspectives therefore emulates the difference between the position of mortals and that of gods.

FOUNDING A NEW CITY
The mission to build a new city is an obsession for Aeneas and the Trojans. In Book II, Aeneas relates the story of Troy's destruction to Dido, who is herself recently displaced and in the process of founding a new city of her own. In Book III, Virgil relates several attempts undertaken by the Trojans to lay the foundations for a city, all of which were thwarted by ill omens or plague. Aeneas also frequently uses the image of the realized city to inspire his people when their spirits flag. The walls, foundation, or towers of a city stand for civilization and order itself, a remedy for the uncertainty, irrationality, and confusion that result from wandering without a home.

VENGEANCE
Avenging a wrong, especially the death of a loved one, is an important element of heroic culture and a pervasive motif in the *Aeneid*. The most prominent instance of vengeance comes in the final lines of the poem. Aeneas, having decided to spare Turnus, changes his mind when reminded of the slain Pallas, whose belt Turnus wears as a trophy. It would be considered dishonorable and disloyal to allow Pallas's death go unpunished. Vengeance comes in other, perhaps less noble, forms as well. Dido's suicide is at least partly an act of revenge on Aeneas, and she curses him as one of her last acts. The

Harpies act out of vengefulness when they curse Aeneas for having killed their livestock. Similarly, the struggles of the gods against one another are likewise motivated by spite and revenge: the history of bruised vanity, left over from Paris's judgment of Venus as the fairest goddess, largely motivates Juno's aggressive behavior against the Trojans and Venus, their divine protector.

SYMBOLS

Symbols are objects, characters, figures, or colors used to represent abstract ideas or concepts.

FLAMES
Fire symbolizes both destruction and erotic desire or love. With images of flames, Virgil connects the two. Paris's desire for Helen eventually leads to the fires of the siege of Troy. When Dido confesses her love for Aeneas to Anna, her sister, she begins, "I recognize / the signs of the old flame, of old desire" (IV.31–32). Dido also recalls her previous marriage in "the thought of the torch and the bridal bed" (IV.25). Torches limit the power of flames by controlling them, but the new love ignited in Dido's heart is never regulated by the institution of marriage, "the bridal bed." The flames she feels do not keep her warm but rather consume her mind. Virgil describes the way she dies in the synonymous terms "enflamed and driven mad" (IV.965).

THE GOLDEN BOUGH
According to the Sibyl, the priestess of Apollo, the golden bough is the symbol Aeneas must carry in order to gain access to the underworld. It is unusual for mortals to be allowed to visit the realm of the dead and then return to life. The golden bough is therefore the sign of Aeneas's special privilege.

THE GATES OF WAR
The opening of these gates indicates a declaration of war in a tradition that was still recognized even in Virgil's own day. That it is Juno rather than a king or even Turnus who opens the gates emphasizes the way immortal beings use mortals to settle scores. The Gates of War thus symbolize the chaos of a world in which divine force, often antagonistic to the health and welfare of mortals, overpowers human will and desire.

THE TROJAN HEARTH GODS

The hearth gods of Troy, or *penates* as they are called in Latin, are mentioned repeatedly throughout the epic. They are symbols of locality and ancestry, tribal gods associated specifically with the city of Troy, who reside in the household hearth. Aeneas gathers them up along with his family when he departs from his devastated home, and they symbolize the continuity of Troy as it is transplanted to a new physical location.

WEATHER

The gods use weather as a force to express their will. The storm that Juno sends at the beginning of the epic symbolizes her rage. Venus, on the other hand, shows her affection for the Trojans by bidding the sea god, Neptune, to protect them. In Book IV, Venus and Juno conspire to isolate Dido and Aeneas in a cave by sending a storm to disrupt their hunting trip, symbolizing the rupture of normal social codes as well. Greek and Roman mythology has a tendency to make its symbols literal in this way—to connect the seen (a storm, for example) with the unseen (divine will) causally and dramatically.

SYMBOLS

SUMMARY & ANALYSIS

BOOK I

> *I sing of warfare and a man at war.*
>
> . . .
>
> *He came to Italy by destiny.* (See QUOTATIONS, p. 59)

Virgil opens his epic poem by declaring its subject, "warfare and a man at war," and asking a muse, or goddess of inspiration, to explain the anger of Juno, queen of the gods (I.1). The man in question is Aeneas, who is fleeing the ruins of his native city, Troy, which has been ravaged in a war with Achilles and the Greeks. The surviving Trojans accompany Aeneas on a perilous journey to establish a new home in Italy, but they must contend with the vindictive Juno.

Juno harbors anger toward Aeneas because Carthage is her favorite city, and a prophecy holds that the race descended from the Trojans will someday destroy Carthage.

Juno holds a permanent grudge against Troy because another Trojan, Paris, judged Juno's rival Venus fairest in a divine beauty contest. Juno calls on Aeolus, the god of the winds, directing him to bring a great storm down upon Aeneas as he sails south of Sicily in search of a friendly harbor. Aeolus obeys, unleashing a fierce storm upon the battle-weary Trojans.

Aeneas watches with horror as the storm approaches. Winds and waves buffet the ships, knocking them off course and scattering them. As the tempest intensifies, Neptune, the god of the sea, senses the presence of the storm in his dominion. He tells the winds that Aeolus has overstepped his bounds and calms the waters just as Aeneas's fleet seems doomed. Seven ships remain, and they head for the nearest land in sight: the coast of Libya. When they reach the shore, before setting out to hunt for food, a weary and worried Aeneas reminds his companions of previous, more deadly adversities they have overcome and the fated end toward which they strive.

Meanwhile, on Mount Olympus, the home of the gods, Aeneas's mother, Venus, observes the Trojans' plight and begs Jupiter, king of the gods, to end their suffering. Jupiter assures her that Aeneas will eventually find his promised home in Italy and that two of Aeneas's descendants, Romulus and Remus, will found the mightiest empire in the world. Jupiter then sends a god down to the people of Carthage to make sure they behave hospitably to the Trojans.

Aeneas remains unaware of the divine machinations that steer his course. While he is in the woods, Venus appears to him in disguise and relates how Dido came to be queen of Carthage. Dido's wealthy husband, Sychaeus, who lived with her in Tyre (a city in Phoenicia, now Syria), was murdered for his gold by Pygmalion, her brother. Sychaeus appeared to Dido as a ghost and advised her to leave Tyre with those who were opposed to the tyrant Pygmalion. She fled, and the emigrant Phoenicians settled across the sea in Libya. They founded Carthage, which has become a powerful city.

Venus advises Aeneas to go into the city and talk to the queen, who will welcome him. Aeneas and his friend Achates approach Carthage, shrouded in a cloud that Venus conjures to prevent them from being seen. On the outskirts of the city, they encounter a shrine to Juno and are amazed to behold a grand mural depicting the events of the Trojan War. Their astonishment increases when they arrive in Dido's court to find many of their comrades who were lost and scattered in the storm asking Dido for aid in rebuilding their fleet. Dido gladly grants their request and says that she wishes she could meet their leader. Achates remarks that he and Aeneas were clearly told the truth regarding their warm welcome, and Aeneas steps forward out of the cloud. Dido is awestruck and delighted to see the famous hero. She invites the Trojan leaders to dine with her in her palace.

Venus worries that Juno will incite the Phoenicians against her son. She sends down another of her sons, Cupid, the god of love, who takes the form of Aeneas's son, Ascanius. In this disguise, Cupid inflames the queen's heart with passion for Aeneas. With love in her eyes, Dido begs Aeneas to tell the story of his adventures during the war and the seven years since he left Troy.

ANALYSIS

Virgil adheres to the epic style that the ancient Greek poet Homer established by invoking the muse at the opening of his poem. A similar invocation begins both the *Iliad* and the *Odyssey*, the Homeric epics that are the models for Virgil's epic, and the *Aeneid* picks up its

subject matter where Homer left off. The events described in the *Aeneid* form a sequel to the *Iliad* and are contemporaneous with the wanderings of Ulysses in the *Odyssey*.

Although Virgil alludes to Homer's epics and self-consciously emulates them, he also attempts to surpass and revise Homer, and the differences between the two authors' epics are important markers of literary evolution. Whereas the *Iliad* and the *Odyssey* call the muse in the first line, Virgil begins the *Aeneid* with the words "I sing," and waits a number of lines before making his invocation. It is as though Virgil is invoking the muse out of obligation rather than out of a genuine belief in divine inspiration. He emphasizes his presence as a narrator and becomes more than a medium through which the epic poem is channeled.

The hero at sea, buffeted by weather and impeded by unexpected encounters, is another recurring motif in epic poetry. According to the Roman worldview, which was derived from the Greeks, men's actions and fortunes are compelled by a unitary fate, and the specific events of their lives are dictated by a host of competing supernatural forces. Aeneas, sailing from the ruins of Troy toward Italy, is not completely in control of his direction and progress. Fate has ordained, we learn, that Aeneas and his people will found a new race in Italy that will eventually become the Roman Empire. Jupiter ensures this outcome, and none of the gods can prevent it from happening. They can, however, affect the *way* in which it happens, and the rivalries and private loyalties of the meddling gods fuel the conflict in the poem.

The reasons for Juno's hatred of the Trojans and her enduring antagonism would have been well known to Virgil's Roman audience, which was familiar with the Greek tradition. Homer details the background of Juno's resentment against Troy in the *Iliad*. The goddess of strife, Eris, threw a golden apple before the goddesses on Olympus and said it was a prize for the most beautiful among them. Three goddesses claimed it: Juno, Venus, and Minerva. They decided to have Paris, a Trojan and the most handsome of mortal men, settle the dispute. In secret, each goddess tried to bribe him, and in the end, he gave the apple to Venus because she offered the most tempting bribe: the fairest woman on Earth, Helen. That Helen was already married to a Greek king named Menelaus only engendered further conflict. When Paris took her away to Troy, her husband assembled the bravest warriors of the Argives (Greeks)— including his brother Agamemnon, Ulysses, and Achilles—and they set sail for Troy, initiating the Trojan War. They laid siege to the city for ten years, and, naturally, the goddesses took sides. Juno and Minerva aided the Greeks, and Venus helped the Trojans, to whom she had an added loyalty since the Trojan warrior Aeneas is her son.

This rivalry between the gods looms over the narrative of the *Aeneid* so heavily that at times the story seems to be less about the deeds of the mortal characters than about the bickering of the gods, who continually disrupt and manipulate events on Earth. One of the *Aeneid*'s main themes, though, is that for both gods and mortals, fate always wins in the end. Aeneas is destined to settle in Italy, and not even the unbridled wrath of Juno, queen of the gods, can prevent this outcome. Jupiter, whose inexorable will is closely identified with fate because he is the highest of the gods, sees to it that his overall plan comes to pass. When Juno has Aeolus torment Aeneas, it is necessary for Jupiter to take sides, so he assists Venus. In fact, Jupiter's occasional intervention on Venus's behalf, to Juno's great frustration, sets the general pattern for the *Aeneid*.

Whereas Juno attempts to defy fate to satisfy her own anger, Aeneas reveals in his first speech in the epic, delivered to his crew upon their landing in Libya, his ability to suppress his own emotions and will in pursuit of his fated duty. Virgil tells us that Aeneas has "contained his anguish" and "feigned hope" in order to rally the morale of his crew by reminding them of past hardships and future glory (I.285–286). He is incapable of emotional self-indulgence. For Aeneas, fate, although promised, demands certain actions and sacrifices. It requires the virtue known as piety, which entails placing his service to fate—his divine mission to found a new city in Italy—above all else in his life.

BOOK II

SUMMARY

> *Did you suppose, my father,*
> *That I could tear myself away and leave you?*
> (See QUOTATIONS, p. 61)

Fulfilling Dido's request, Aeneas begins his sorrowful story, adding that retelling it entails reexperiencing the pain. He takes us back to ten years into the Trojan War: at the moment the tale begins, the Danaans (Greeks) have constructed a giant wooden horse with a hollow belly. They secretly hide their best soldiers, fully armed, within the horse, while the rest of the Greek army lies low some distance from Troy. The sight of a massive horse standing before their gates on an apparently deserted battlefield baffles the Trojans.

Near the horse, the Trojans find a Greek youth named Sinon. He explains that the Greeks have wished to flee Troy for some time but were prevented by fierce storms. A prophet told them to sacrifice one of their own, and Sinon was chosen. But Sinon managed to escape during the preparations, and the Greeks left him behind. The Trojans show him pity and ask the meaning of the great horse. Sinon says that it was an offering to the goddess Minerva, who turned against the Greeks after the desecration of one of her temples by Ulysses. Sinon claims that if any harm comes to the wooden statue, Troy will be destroyed by Minerva's wrath, but if the Trojans install the horse within their city walls, they will rise victorious in war against southern Greece, like a tidal wave, with Minerva on their side.

Aeneas continues his story: after Sinon finishes speaking, two giant serpents rise up from the sea and devour the Trojan priest Laocoön and his two sons as punishment for hurling a spear at the horse. The snakes then slither up to the shrine of Minerva. The Trojans interpret the snakes' attack as an omen that they must appease Minerva, so they wheel the horse into the city of Troy.

Night falls, and while the city sleeps, Sinon opens the horse's belly, releasing the Greek warriors. The warriors kill the Trojan guards and open the gates of the city to the rest of their forces. Meanwhile, Hector, the fallen leader of the Trojan army, appears to Aeneas in a dream and informs him that the city has been infiltrated. Climbing to his roof, Aeneas sees fighting everywhere and Troy in flames. He runs for arms and then heads for the heart of the city, joined by a few of his men.

Aeneas and his men surprise and kill many Greeks, but are too badly outnumbered to make a difference. Eventually they go to King Priam's palace, where a battle is brewing. The Greeks, led by Pyrrhus, break into the palace. Pyrrhus kills Polites, the young son of Priam and Hecuba, and then slaughters Priam on his own altar.

Aeneas continues relating his story: nearly overcome with grief over this slaughter, he sees Helen, the cause of the war, hiding. He determines to kill her, but Venus appears and explains that blame for the war belongs with the gods, not Helen. Venus advises Aeneas to flee Troy at once, since his fate is elsewhere. Aeneas then proceeds to the house of his father, Anchises, but Anchises refuses to leave. But after omens appear—first a harmless tongue of flame on Ascanius's forehead, then a bright falling star in the sky—Anchises is persuaded to flee the city.

Aeneas takes his father on his back and flees with his wife, Creusa, his son, Ascanius, and many other followers. Unfortunately, in the commotion Creusa is lost from the group. After everyone exits the city, Aeneas returns to search for her, but instead he meets her shade, or spirit. She tells him not to be sorrowful because a new home and wife await him in Hesperia. Somewhat comforted, Aeneas leaves Troy burning and leads the survivors into the mountains.

ANALYSIS

With Aeneas's claim that his tale of Troy's fall is so sorrowful that it would bring tears even to the eyes of a soldier as harsh as Ulysses, Virgil calls attention to his own act of retelling the Trojan horse episode from a new angle, that of the vanquished Trojans. In Homer's *Iliad* and *Odyssey*, we learn the story of the Trojan War from the perspective of Ulysses and the Greeks. Virgil's claim is that even the Greeks, the victors, would be able to feel the sorrow of the event if it were told properly from the point of view of the victims. Virgil writes a characteristically evenhanded account, so that both losers and winners earn our sympathy and respect.

Virgil tries to minimize the humiliation of the Trojans and of his hero, Aeneas. He makes sure that Aeneas does not appear to be less of a warrior than the Greeks, even though they defeated him. When Aeneas admits that the Trojans were duped by the wooden horse trick, Virgil tempers the failure by emphasizing that not all Trojans were fooled. Aeneas's mention that some Trojans counseled the others to destroy the horse demonstrates that there was in fact a degree of wisdom and perhaps even foresight among the Trojan people. He also carefully recounts all the details by which they were persuaded and frightened—the lies of the young Greek and the sign of the serpents, which gobbled up Laocoön, the man who had most vocally protested bringing the horse inside the city—in order to show that the Trojan fear of offending the gods was valid. In the end, the Trojans bring the horse into their city not out of foolishness but out of a legitimate and even honorable respect for the gods. Against Aeneas's description of the Trojans' earnest reverence, the Greeks begin to look guilty of bad sportsmanship.

At points during his story, Aeneas emphasizes the irrelevance of mortal concerns in the face of divine will. Venus's persuasion of Aeneas to not kill Helen, for instance, relies on the ultimate inability of mortals to influence their destinies. Venus tells him to hold neither Helen nor Paris responsible for Troy's downfall: he must realize that "the harsh will of the gods" (II.792) caused Troy's destruction. Venus's words reveal that although Aeneas and the Trojans lose a battle with the Greeks that they might have won, in the end they have no choice but to submit to the unfavorable will of the gods. But the gods' will is also what enables some of the Trojans to escape from Troy. Again, fate must always be fulfilled: Aeneas is destined to survive. His sufferings in Troy are to be redeemed, eventually, by his glory in Italy. The shade of his wife, Creusa, comforts him with this message, and following his encounter with Creusa's shade, Aeneas keeps his foretold destiny always in mind, distant though this destiny may seem.

BOOK III

SUMMARY

Aeneas continues his story, recounting the aftermath of the fall of Troy. After escaping from Troy, he leads the survivors to the coast of Antander, where they build a new fleet of ships. They sail first to Thrace, where Aeneas prepares to offer sacrifices. When he tears at the roots and branches of a tree, dark blood soaks the ground and the bark. The tree speaks to him, revealing itself to be the spirit of Polydorus, son of Priam. Priam had sent Polydorus to the king of Thrace to be safe from the war, but when Troy fell, the Thracian king sided with the Greeks and killed Polydorus.

After holding a funeral for Polydorus, Aeneas and the Trojans embark from Thrace with a sense of dread at the Thracian violation of the ethics of hospitality. They sail southward to the holy island of Delos. At Delos, Apollo speaks to Aeneas, instructing him to go to the land of his ancestors. Anchises interprets Apollo's remark as a reference to the island of Crete, where one of the great Trojan forefathers—Teucrus, after whom the Trojans are sometimes called Teucrians—had long ago ruled.

Aeneas and his group sail to Crete and began to build a new city, but a terrible plague soon strikes. The gods of Troy appear to Aeneas in a dream and explain that his father is mistaken: the ancestral land to which Apollo referred is not Crete but Italy, the original home of Dardanus, from whom the Trojans take the name Dardanians. These hearth gods also reassert the prophecy of Roman supremacy, declaring, "You must prepare great walls for a great race" (III.223).

The Trojan refugees take to the sea again. A cover of black storm clouds hinders them. They land at the Strophades, islands of the Harpies, fierce bird-creatures with feminine faces. The Trojans slaughter many cows and goats that are roaming free and hold a feast, provoking an attack from the Harpies. To no avail, the Trojans attempt to fight the Harpies off, and one of the horrible creatures places a curse upon them. Confirming that they are destined for Italy, she prophesies that the Trojans will not establish their city until hunger forces them to try to eat their very tables.

Disturbed by the episode, the Trojans depart for the island of Leucata, where they make offerings at a shrine to Apollo. Next, they set sail in the direction of Italy until they reach Buthrotum, in Chaonia. There, Aeneas is astonished to discover that Helenus, one of Priam's sons, has become king of a Greek city. Helenus and Andromachë had been taken by Pyrrhus as war prizes, but seized power over part of their captor's kingdom after he was killed.

Aeneas meets Andromachë and she relates the story of her and Helenus's captivity. Helenus then arrives and advises Aeneas on the path ahead. Andromachë adds that to reach the western coast of Italy it is necessary to take the long way around Sicily, to the south. The short path, a narrow gap of water between Sicily and Italy, is rendered practically impossible to navigate by two potentially lethal hazards: Charybdis, a whirlpool, and Scylla, a six-headed monster.

Following Andromachë's instructions, Aeneas pilots his fleet along the southern coast of Italy to Sicily, where Mount Etna is erupting in the distance. Resting on a beach, the Trojans are startled by a ragged stranger who begs to be taken aboard. He was in the Greek army under Ulysses, and his crew was captured by a giant Cyclops on Sicily and barely escaped alive. He reports that Ulysses stabbed the monster in his one eye to allow their escape.

As the stranger finishes telling the Trojans his tale, the blinded Cyclops nearly stumbles upon the group. The Trojans make a quick escape with the Greek straggler, just as the other Cyclopes come down to the shore. Sailing around Sicily, they pass several recognizable landmarks before landing at Drepanum, where Aeneas endures yet another unexpected loss: his father's death.

Aeneas turns to Dido and concludes his story by saying that divine will has driven him to her shores.

ANALYSIS

Although we know from Book I that the Trojans have been wandering for seven years, Aeneas, in telling his story, gives little explicit indication of the passage of time. Instead, the time frame is revealed in an indirect way by the situations the Trojan refugees encounter on their journey. In Book I, we see that there is already a mural in Carthage picturing the events of the Trojan War by the time Aeneas's crew arrives there. Historically, the Trojan War and the founding of Carthage were separated by centuries, not years, though the epic tradition has compressed this time span. We also see Helenus and Andromachë, in a moment that comes even before Aeneas's arrival in Carthage, and we learn that Pyrrhus, whom we last saw killing Priam, is now dead himself. Such details give us a sense that greater lengths of time have passed than the seafaring hero's description of his various arrivals and departures can convey.

Aeneas's path across the Mediterranean is not straight, and his fleet is frequently thrown off course or sent backtracking by the gods. He has to wait for summer before he can even set off from the coast of Antander, outside of Troy, and he must wait for auspicious weather each time he takes to the sea. Aeneas indicates the length of time he spends on Crete, where the Trojans actually begin to establish a new city, when he describes the period as "a year of death" (III.195). Such lengthy stops account for the passage of so many years between the departure of the refugees from Troy, on the coast of Asia Minor, and their landfall in Libya, near Carthage.

By the end of Book III, we have heard the prophecy that Aeneas is destined to found the race that will become the Roman people reiterated several times, each time with some additional—and often ambiguous—information. Aeneas's fate is set, but Virgil makes the role of fate complex, so that his hero's success in each adventure does not always seem a foregone conclusion. The dangers that Aeneas and his crew encounter are real threats, even if we know that he will survive them.

The Trojan destiny is more flexible and alterable than it might seem, at least in a limited sense. There is no set time span that binds the workings of fate regarding Aeneas or prevents considerable delays on the way to Italy. The gods, who know what fate ultimately holds for Aeneas, still try to alter his path, knowing that they can assist him or cause him suffering along the way. It becomes obvious, in the case of the Harpy's curse, that the actions of the Trojans themselves, and not only those of the gods, can affect what they will have to endure. The fleeing Trojans, in a sense, try to take the easy way out—they keep looking for the nearest place to settle and make a new life. This urgent craving for stability is probably what causes Anchises to misinterpret Apollo's message, when he steers the group south from Delos to nearby Crete instead of Italy. In the end, though, Virgil's message is that fate is inevitable and demands obedience. The more one tries to delay or avoid fate, the more one suffers. At every wrong turn Aeneas and his men take, they endure another hardship that eventually puts them back on the path to Italy.

A general overview of what happens to some of the major figures of the Trojan War after the fall of Troy is helpful in understanding some of the references in Book III. Pyrrhus the Greek, son of Achilles, took back two Trojans to be his slaves: Helenus, son of Priam, and Andromachë, widow of Hector. Helenus and Andromachë were soon married, though the latter continued to mourn Hector, her lost husband. Pyrrhus married Hermione, the daughter of Menelaus and Helen, born before Helen was taken to Troy. Unfortunately for Pyrrhus, Hermione had already been betrothed to Orestes, the son of Agamemnon. Orestes came and killed Pyrrhus, whose kingdom fell to Helenus. Thus, Helenus and Andromachë came to be rulers of a Greek city. This whole series of events is described in the *Oresteia*, a famous trilogy of plays by Aeschylus. As for the other Greek generals, Menelaus and Ulysses were both forced to delay their homecomings as punishment for wrongs committed in the sacking of Troy. Menelaus took eight years to return to Sparta, while Ulysses did not reach Ithaca for ten long years, as recounted by Homer in the *Odyssey*. Virgil solidifies the link between these stories by having Aeneas stop on the shore of Sicily, right where the Greeks had stopped, and actually encounter a member of Ulysses' crew who was left behind.

BOOK IV

SUMMARY

The flame of love for Aeneas that Cupid has lit in Dido's heart only grows while she listens to his sorrowful tale. She hesitates, though, because after the death of her husband, Sychaeus, she swore that she would never marry again. On the other hand, as her sister Anna counsels her, by marrying Aeneas she would increase the might of Carthage, because many Trojan warriors follow Aeneas. For the moment, consumed by love, Dido allows the work of city building to fall by the wayside.

Juno sees Dido's love for Aeneas as a way to keep Aeneas from going to Italy. Pretending to make a peace offering, Juno suggests to Venus that they find a way to get Dido and Aeneas alone together. If they marry, Juno suggests, the Trojans and the Tyrians would be at peace, and she and Venus would end their feud. Venus knows Juno is just trying to keep the Trojans from Italy but allows Juno to go ahead anyway.

One day when Dido, her court, and Aeneas are out hunting, Juno brings a storm down upon them to send the group scrambling for shelter and arranges for Aeneas and Dido to wind up in a cave by themselves. They make love in the cave and live openly as lovers when they return to Carthage. Dido considers them to be married though the union has yet to be consecrated in ceremony. Anxious rumors spread that Dido and Aeneas have surrendered themselves entirely to lust and have begun to neglect their responsibilities as rulers.

When Jupiter learns of Dido and Aeneas's affair, he dispatches Mercury to Carthage to remind Aeneas that his destiny lies elsewhere and that he must leave for Italy. This message shocks Aeneas—he must obey, but he does not know how to tell Dido of his departure. He tries to prepare his fleet to set sail in secret, but the queen suspects his ploy and confronts him. In a rage, she insults him and accuses him of stealing her honor. While Aeneas pities her, he maintains that he has no choice but to follow the will of the gods: "I sail for Italy not of my own free will" (IV.499). As a last effort, Dido sends Anna to try to persuade the Trojan hero to stay, but to no avail.

Dido writhes between fierce love and bitter anger. Suddenly, she appears calm and instructs Anna to build a great fire in the courtyard. There, Dido says, she can rid Aeneas from her mind by burning all the clothes and weapons he has left behind and even the bed they slept on. Anna obeys, not realizing that Dido is in fact planning her own death—by making the fire her own funeral pyre. As night falls, Dido's grief leaves her sleepless. Aeneas does sleep, but in his dreams, Mercury visits him again to tell him that he has delayed too long already and must leave at once. Aeneas awakens and calls his men to the ships, and they set sail.

Dido sees the fleet leaving and falls into her final despair. She can no longer bear to live. Running out to the courtyard, she climbs upon the pyre and unsheathes a sword Aeneas has left behind. She throws herself upon the blade and with her last words curses her absent lover. As Anna and the servants run up to the dying queen, Juno takes pity on Dido and ends her suffering and her life.

ANALYSIS

Although her relationship with Aeneas spans only this one book of the *Aeneid*, Dido has become a literary icon for the tragic lover, like Shakespeare's Romeo and Juliet. Though at times Aeneas's happiness in his love for Dido seems to equal hers, it is with considerably less grief and anxiety that he is able to leave her in Carthage and go back about the business of bringing the survivors of Troy to Italy and founding Rome. Whereas Dido not only loves Aeneas but hopes he and his warriors will strengthen her city, Aeneas's actions are the result of a momentary abandonment of his true duties and responsibilities. He indulges temporarily in romance and the pleasures of the flesh, but when Jupiter, through Mercury, reminds Aeneas of his destiny, he is dutiful and ready to resume his mission.

When Aeneas says good-bye to Dido, we see two sides to the hero as in Book I, when he hides his worries to appear brave before his crew. Aeneas's statement that he is forced to sail to Italy and Virgil's remark that Aeneas "struggle[s] with desire to calm and comfort [Dido] in all her pain" demonstrate Aeneas's conflicted nature (IV.546–547). He piously carries out the duties allotted him by fate; though he feels emotions and experiences desires, he is powerless to act on them. From Virgil's perspective, Aeneas is not heartless, as Dido thinks him, but merely capable of subordinating matters of the heart to the demands of duty. Aeneas's reminder to Dido that they were never officially married suggests, somewhat dubiously, that had they entered into such an ordained commitment he would not leave. But, he argues, without a true marriage, he is sacrificing only his own desires by leaving Dido.

Virgil treats love as he treats the gods—as an outside force acting upon mortals, not a function of the individual's free will or innate identity. He does not idealize love; rather, he associates it with imagery linked to madness, fire, or disease, presenting love as a force that acts on Dido with a violence that is made literal by the end of Book IV in her suicide. Virgil's language in the first lines of the book indicates that Dido's emotions corrode her self-control; he describes her love as "inward fire eating her away" (IV.3). Later, Dido's decision to have a funeral pyre erected and then kill herself upon it returns to this imagery, and Virgil compares Dido's suicide to a city taken over by enemies, "As though . . . / . . . / Flames billowed on the roofs of men and gods" (IV.927–929). Cupid's arrow, shot to promote love between Aeneas and Dido, causes hatred, death, and destruction.

Love is at odds with law and fate, as it distracts its victims from their responsibilities. While with Aeneas, Dido abandons her construction of Carthage. She even admits to Aeneas that her own subjects have grown to hate her because of her selfish actions. Aeneas, too, must move on because the time he spends with Dido only keeps him from his selfless task of founding an empire.

In the *Aeneid,* civic responsibility resides with the male. An attitude that might be termed misogynistic seeps into Virgil's descriptions of Juno and even Dido. Aeneas's dream-vision of Mercury articulates this sentiment: "woman's a thing / forever fitful and forever changing" (IV.792–793). Virgil clearly enjoys making Juno look foolish, and he also likes to depict Juno's vain efforts in comic terms as a domestic quarrel—a battle of wills between husband and wife played out before an audience that knows Jupiter has the power in the divine family. Dido also shows herself to be less responsible than her partner. Whereas Dido kills herself for love, leaving the city she founded without a leader, Aeneas returns to his course, guiding the refugees of a lost city to the foundation of a new city.

BOOK V

SUMMARY

Massive storm clouds greet the Trojan fleet as it embarks from Carthage, hindering the approach to Italy. Aeneas redirects the ships to the Sicilian port of Eryx, where his friend and fellow Trojan Acestes rules. After landing and being welcomed by Acestes, Aeneas realizes that it is the one-year anniversary of his father's death. He proposes eight days of sacrificial offerings and a ninth day of competitive games, including rowing, running, javelin, and boxing, in honor of his father.

When the ninth day arrives, the festivities begin with a rowing race. Four galleys participate, each piloted by one of Aeneas's captains and manned by many eager youths. A suitable distance is marked off along the coastline and the race starts, with many spectators cheering from the beaches. Gyas, piloting the ship *Chimaera,* leads during the first half of the race. But at the turnaround point, his helmsman takes the turn too wide, and his boat falls behind. Down the final stretch, Sergestus takes the lead, but plows into the rocks. Colanthus and Mnestheus race together to the finish, but Colanthus prays to Neptune, who causes him to win. Lavish prizes are bestowed upon the competitors—even upon Sergestus, after he dislodges his ship from the rocks.

Next comes the footrace. Nisus leads for most of the way, but slips on sacrificial blood near the finish. Euryalus wins the race, but Aeneas, as generous as before, hands out prizes to all the competitors. Next, the mighty Trojan Dares puts on his gauntlets (heavy fighting gloves) and challenges anyone to box with him. No one rises to the challenge at first, but Acestes finally persuades his fellow Sicilian Entellus—a great boxer now past his prime—to step into the ring. They begin the match, pounding each other with fierce blows. Younger and more agile, Dares darts quicker than Entellus. When he dodges a punch from Entellus, Entellus tumbles to the ground. Entellus gets up, though, and attacks Dares with such fierceness that Aeneas decides to call an end to the match. Entellus backs off, but to show what he could have done to Dares, he kills a bull—the prize—with a single devastating punch that spills the beast's brains.

Next, the archery contest commences. Eurytion wins by shooting a dove out of the sky, but Acestes causes a spectacular stir when his arrow miraculously catches fire in midair. Finally, the youths of Troy and Sicily ride out on horseback to demonstrate their technique. They charge at each other in a mock battle exercise, impressing their fathers with their skill and audacity.

Meanwhile, Juno's anger against the Trojans has not subsided. She dispatches Iris, her messenger, down to the Trojan women, who are further along the beach from where the men enjoy their sport. Iris stirs them to riot, playing on their fear of further journey and more battles. She distributes flaming torches among them, inciting them to burn the Trojan ships so that the men will be forced to build their new city here, in Sicily. Persuaded, the angry women set fire to the fleet. The Trojan men see the smoke and rush up the beach. They douse the ships with water but fail to extinguish the flames. Finally,

Aeneas prays to Jupiter to preserve the fleet, and immediately a rainstorm hits, ending the conflagration.

The incident shakes Aeneas, and he ponders whether he should be satisfied with settling in peace on the Sicilian coast. His friend Nautes, a seer, offers better advice: they should leave some Trojans—the old, the frail, the injured, and the women weary of sailing—in the care of Acestes. Aeneas considers this plan, and that night the ghost of his father appears to him, advising him to listen to Nautes. The spirit also tells him that Aeneus is going to have to fight a difficult foe in Latium, but must first visit the underworld to speak more with Anchises.

Aeneas does not know the meaning of his father's mysterious prediction, but the next day he describes it to Acestes, who consents to host those who do not wish to continue to Italy after the Trojan fleet departs. Venus, fearing more tricks from Juno, worries about the group's safety at sea. She pleads with Neptune to let Aeneas reach Italy without harm. Neptune agrees to allow them safe passage across the waters, demanding, however, that one of the crew perish on the voyage, as a sort of sacrifice for the others. On the voyage, Palinurus, the lead captain of Aeneas's fleet, falls asleep at the helm and falls into the sea.

ANALYSIS

Neptune's last strike at Palinurus seems a ridiculous impulse of divine vanity: Neptune harbors no explicit anger against the Trojans and has no interest in delaying their destiny, yet he requires the death of Palinurus as a price for safe passage. It is unclear why Neptune needs to be pacified at all—he is calm and gentle in his talk with Venus. They conduct their dealings with the tone of a friendly business transaction, and the bloodshed incurred seems gratuitous and irrational, demonstrating yet again how the whims of the gods have grave consequences for mortal affairs.

The games on the shores of Eryx serve as a diversion both for us and for Aeneas and his crew. After four books of foul weather, destruction, suffering, and suicide, sport provides a lighthearted interlude. The games provide comic moments, as when Gyas gets stuck in the shoals and tosses his helmsman overboard, or when Nisus, in order to throw the race for his friend, Euryalus, slips on blood during the footrace, putting himself in the path of Salius. Such moments of lightness are rare in the *Aeneid;* Virgil fairly consistently maintains a solemn tone. In addition to providing comic relief, these sequences allow Virgil to display his poetic skill in creating excitement and suspense. He uses interjections and imperatives to draw us into the races:

> But close upon him, look,
> Diores in his flight matched stride for stride,
> Nearing his shoulder.　　　(V.412–414)

Virgil does not often break from the formal, epic style associated with the genre of tragedy, but this style does not always encompass the range of emotions that he wishes to portray. Above all, Virgil excels at representing universal passions, and here he portrays the passion for sport and physical competition. Any athlete can relate to the comic frustration of the losers, the triumphant gloating of the winners, the fervent displays of masculinity, and the irreverent enthusiasm of the spectators. The games matter little to the plot as a whole, but they show a more lighthearted facet of Virgil's artistry—one that is welcome after Dido's suicide, one of the epic's darkest passages.

The goddesses Juno and Venus continue their quarrel by meddling further in the journey of the weary Trojans. The gods, not the hero, drive the plot—Aeneas has been reduced to a responsive role. A low point in terms of morale occurs when, to stop the burning of his fleet, Aeneas begs Jupiter to help him or end his life. Virgil's hero has reached the limit of psychological suffering in the face of divine mistreatment that he perceives to be arbitrary. That Aeneas goes so far as to consider ignoring the fates and settling in Sicily simply to end this weary journey indicates how tired and perhaps powerless he feels. But the importance of stoic persistence is one of the *Aeneid*'s messages, and Aeneas decides to go on, his strength renewed by the visit of Anchises' spirit.

BOOK VI

SUMMARY

Roman, remember by your strength to rule

. . .

To spare the conquered, battle down the proud.
(See QUOTATIONS, p. 62)

At last, the Trojan fleet arrives on the shores of Italy. The ships drop anchor off the coast of Cumae, near modern-day Naples. Following his father's instructions, Aeneas makes for the Temple of Apollo, where the Sibyl, a priestess, meets him. She commands him to make his request. Aeneas prays to Apollo to allow the Trojans to settle in Latium. The priestess warns him that more trials await in Italy: fighting on the scale of the Trojan War, a foe of the caliber of the Greek warrior Achilles, and further interference from Juno. Aeneas inquires whether the Sibyl can gain him entrance to Dis, so that he might visit his father's spirit as directed. The Sibyl informs him that to enter Dis with any hope of returning, he must first have a sign. He must find a golden branch in the nearby forest. She instructs him that if the bough breaks off the tree easily, it means fate calls Aeneas to the underworld. If Aeneas is not meant to travel there, the bough will not come off the tree.

Aeneas looks in dismay at the size of the forest, but after he says a prayer, a pair of doves descends and guides him to the desired tree, from which he manages to tear the golden branch. The hero returns to the priestess with the token, and she leads him to the gate of Dis.

Just inside the gate runs the river Acheron. The ferryman Charon delivers the spirits of the dead across the river; however, Aeneas notices that some souls are refused passage and must remain on the near bank. The Sibyl explains that these are the souls of dead people whose corpses have not received proper burial. With great sadness, Aeneas spots Palinurus among the undelivered. Charon explains to the visitors that no living bodies may cross the river, but the Sibyl shows him the golden branch. Appeased, Charon ferries them across. On the other side, Aeneas stands aghast, hearing the wailing of thousands of suffering souls. The spirits of the recently deceased line up before Minos for judgment.

Nearby are the Fields of Mourning, where suicides wander. There, Aeneas sees Dido. Surprised and saddened, he speaks to her, with some regret, claiming that he left her not of his own will. The shade of the dead queen turns away from him toward the shade of her husband, Sychaeus, and Aeneas sheds tears of pity.

Aeneas continues to the field of war heroes, where he sees many casualties of the Trojan War. The Greeks flee at first sight of him. The Sibyl urges Aeneas onward, and they pass an enormous fortress. Inside the fortress, Rhadamanthus doles out judgments upon the most evil of sinners, and terrible tortures are carried out. Finally, Aeneas and the Sibyl come to the Blessed Groves, where the good wander about in peace and comfort. At last, Aeneas sees his father. Anchises greets him warmly and congratulates him on having made the difficult journey. He gladly answers some of Aeneas's many questions, regarding such issues as how the dead are dispersed in Dis and how good souls can eventually reach the Fields of Gladness. But with little time at hand, Anchises presses on to the reason for Aeneas's journey to the underworld—the explication of his lineage in Italy. Anchises describes what will become of the Trojan descendants: Romulus will found Rome, a Caesar will eventually come from the line of Ascanius, and Rome will reach a Golden Age of rule over the world. Finally, Aeneas grasps the profound significance of his long journey to Italy. Anchises accompanies Aeneas out of Dis, and Aeneas returns to his comrades on the beach. At once, they pull up anchor and move out along the coast.

ANALYSIS

Aeneas's journey to the underworld in Book VI is another of the *Aeneid*'s most famous passages. In fact, this passage helped raise Virgil to the status of a Christian prophet in the Middle Ages. In the fourteenth century, the Italian poet Dante used it as the foundation for his journey through hell in the *Inferno*, even though Virgil's version of the afterlife was obviously not a Christian one. Like Virgil, for example, Dante designed a hell with many sections and in which more severe punishments are handed down to those with greater sins. Also like Virgil, Dante exercised his formidable imagination in inventing penalties for sinners. While Virgil's Dis is pre-Christian, it represents an advanced version of classical theology, which was not codified in the way that modern religions are. In a world of temperamental gods who demand sacrifice and seem to dispense punishments and rewards almost arbitrarily, Virgil portrays an afterlife in which people are judged according to the virtue of their lives on

Earth. This scheme of the afterlife is an idea that Christianity fused with the Judaic tradition into the Western consciousness centuries later, but that has its sources in the Orphic mysteries of classical antiquity. The presence of Orpheus, "priest of Thrace," in the Blessed Groves confirms the influence of Orphism, which was also a source for Plato's views of the afterlife, on Virgil's vision of the land of shades.

Rhadamanthus's practice of listening to sinners and then sentencing them is remarkably similar to the Christian conception of judgment after death: souls who fail to repent for their sins on Earth pay more dearly for them in hell. Of course, one major difference is that Virgil does not have a separate equivalent of Christian heaven. All souls migrate to Dis, and the good ones occupy a better place, the Fields of Gladness, within the grand dungeon. However, in a way this scheme still fits with Christian theology, which postulates that before Christ's death and resurrection, all souls—good or bad—went to hell. To a Christian mindset, then, it was theologically accurate for Virgil, who died nineteen years before Christ's birth, to place even the good souls in Dis. Though this connection may seem tenuous to us, Virgil's influence among Christian poets and scholars increased because of these affinities.

Aeneas's trip to the underworld is also Virgil's opportunity to indulge in an extensive account of Rome's future glory, particularly in his glorification of the Caesars. Virgil renders Augustus—his own ruler and benefactor—the epitome of the Roman Empire, the promised ruler who presides over the Golden Age. That Augustus was a patron of Virgil should not necessarily cause us to dismiss these passages as pure propaganda, however. Virgil had good reason to think he was living at the high point of history—after all, Rome ruled most of the known world and seemed invincible. In this context, Augustus emerges as the natural counterpart to Aeneas, bringing to perfect fruition the city whose history the Trojan hero initiated.

BOOK VII

SUMMARY

Amata tossed and turned . . .

. . .

While the infection first, like dew of poison
Fallen on her, pervaded all her senses.

(See QUOTATIONS, p. 63)

Sailing up the coast of Italy, the Trojans reach the mouth of the Tiber River, near the kingdom of Latium. Virgil, invoking the muse once again to kick off the second half of his epic narrative, describes the political state of affairs in Latium. The king, Latinus, has a single daughter, Lavinia. She is pursued by many suitors, but the great warrior Turnus, lord of a nearby kingdom, appears most eligible for her hand. Worried by a prophet's prediction that a foreign army will conquer the kingdom, Latinus consults the Oracle of Faunus. A strange voice from the oracle instructs the king that his daughter should marry a foreigner, not a Latin.

Meanwhile, Aeneas and his captains are eating on the beach, with fruit spread out on flat, hard loaves of bread. They finish the fruit but are still hungry, so they eat the bread that they have used as tables. Ascanius notes with a laugh that they have indeed eaten their tables, thus fulfilling the Harpies' curse in a manner less dire than anticipated. Aeneas recognizes that they have arrived at their promised land. The next day, he sends emissaries to King Latinus, requesting a share of the land for the foundation of a new city. Latinus offers territory as well as something extra—mindful of the oracle's words, he suggests that Aeneas take the hand of Lavinia in matrimony. Latinus recognizes that accepting fate, even if it means that the Trojans will one day rule his kingdom, proves a safer course than resisting destiny.

Juno, however, still has not exhausted her anger against the Trojans. Unable to keep them from Italian shores forever, she vows at least to delay the foundation of their city and to cause them more suffering. She dispatches Allecto, one of the Furies, to Latium to rouse anger on the part of the natives against the Trojans. First, Allecto infects Queen Amata, Latinus's wife, causing her to oppose the marriage of Lavinia and Aeneas. Virgil describes Allecto's rousing of Amata's anger with the metaphor of a snake that twists and winds itself around Amata's body. Then Allecto approaches Turnus and inflames him with indignation at the idea of losing Lavinia and submitting to a Trojan king.

Turnus assembles his army and prepares to drive the Trojans out of Italy. Shepherds prove the first to bear arms. As a result of Juno's meddling, Ascanius sets off to hunt in the woods and fells a stag that happens to be a favorite pet of Latinus's herdsman. The animal staggers back to his master before dying. The herdsman summons the other shepherds to track down the hunter, and the Trojans, sensing a commotion, come to Ascanius's aid. Many Latins are slain in a brief skirmish, then each side retreats temporarily. The shepherds go before King Latinus, carrying the dead, and plead with him to launch an all-out assault on the Trojans. Latinus does not wish to engage in battle, but all the court—even his own wife—clamor for war. In the end, he throws up his hands and retreats to his chambers, feeling unable to stop what the gods have set in motion. Turnus amasses a great army, captained by the greatest warriors in Italy, and marches them to war.

ANALYSIS

The Trojans' landing in Latium begins the epic's second half. The *Aeneid* demands comparison to the epics of Homer: whereas the first half of Virgil's epic—a chronicle of the wanderings of Aeneas and his crew in the wake of the fall of Troy—takes up the themes of the *Odyssey,* the second six books share the martial themes of the *Iliad*. In these later books, Virgil describes the strife that leads to the unification of the Latin peoples. Virgil's second invocation to the muse marks this division. Beginning in Book VII, Virgil dwells with more careful attention on the geography of the region he describes. He knows that these locations are familiar to his contemporary Roman audience, and will reinforce their sense of historical connection to the legendary events of the narrative.

Virgil also incorporates an interesting element of Roman lore into the beginning of the war between the Latins and Trojans. Historically, whenever the Romans prepared to march into battle against an enemy, they would open the Gates of War—enormous gates of brass and iron that were constructed as a tribute to Mars, the god of war. Opening these gates, they believed themselves to be releasing the Furies, who inflame the hearts of soldiers and drive them into the fray with a passion for death—the polytheistic version of a battle cry. Virgil claims that this tradition already existed in the time of Aeneas. Generally, the king opens the gates, but since Latinus is unwilling—as he has opposed the war from the start—Juno descends to open the gates herself. At this moment, Turnus, whom the Fury Allecto has already infected with bloodlust, gathers his company to march out and confront the Trojans.

Even though Juno openly admits for the first time that she cannot win, she persists in her defiance of the fates. She cannot prevent the Trojans from founding a new city, yet she remains fixed in her determination to inflict suffering on them. She says:

> It will not be permitted me—so be it—
> To keep the man from rule in Italy;
> By changeless fate Lavinia waits, his bride.
> And yet to drag it out, to pile delay
> Upon delay in these great matters—that
> I can do: to destroy both countries' people,
> That I can do.   (VII.427–433)

At this point in the narrative, Virgil has imparted Juno with base emotions that, in their extremity, seem beyond human capacity. Her obsession with revenge drives her to hurt Aeneas, though she acknowledges the futility of the violence she incites with phrases such as "[i]t will not be permitted me" and "changeless fate." For Juno, thwarting the Trojans is no longer a matter of control but rather of pride, as her resolute assertion, "That I can do," makes clear. Virgil's Juno, a fearsome, self-important, and vengeful character from the start, reaches the height of her anger in this passage and appears pathetic in her willful obstruction of fated events.

BOOK VIII

SUMMARY

While Turnus gathers his forces, Aeneas readies the Trojan troops and solicits support from nearby cities in Latium. Still, he is troubled at his prospects in battle. That night, the river god Tiberinus speaks to him and tells him to approach and form an alliance with the Arcadians, who are also at war with the Latins. Aeneas takes two galleys and rows several days up the Tiber to the forest of the Arcadians. There, the Trojans address the Arcadian king, Evander,

who gladly offers aid against their common enemy and invites Aeneas to a feast.

After the feast, holy rites are performed in honor of Hercules, the patron of the Arcadians, who killed the monster Cacus near where Arcadia now stands. Evander also explains how Saturn descended to Italy long ago and formed a nation from the wild savages who inhabited the land, calling it Latium. The Arcadians still dwell in relative simplicity. Even Evander boasts only a small house but offers everything at his disposal to Aeneas in hospitality.

Meanwhile, Venus frets over Aeneas's upcoming war. She speaks to her husband, Vulcan, the god of fire and forging, and persuades him to make Aeneas new weapons and armor that will give him an added advantage. Vulcan commands his workers—Cyclopes inside the great volcano Etna—to begin forging the items.

The next morning, back in Arcadia, King Evander assigns what troops he can spare to Aeneas's command. He also bids neighboring kingdoms to send their aid. All told, several thousand soldiers are rallied to accompany the Trojans back to the front, but due to their increased numbers, they must march rather than row, which causes a delay. Finally, Evander dispatches Pallas, his own son, and requests that Aeneas teach Pallas the arts of war and return him home in safety.

The new army marches all day. At the camp that night, Venus suddenly appears to Aeneas and presents him with the arms that Vulcan has completed: helmet, corselet, sword, spear, and shield, all of them beautifully crafted and stronger than metal forged by humans. The face of the shield is particularly notable, for on it Vulcan has depicted the story of the Roman glory that awaits Italy. Aeneas sees Romulus being nursed by the she-wolf, the defeat of the Gauls, Caesar Augustus as he defeats Antony and Cleopatra at the battle of Actium, and much else.

SUMMARY & ANALYSIS

ANALYSIS

After many books in which we see Aeneas being alternately tormented at the hands of Juno and rescued by Venus and her allies, the fates begin to balance out. A veritable coalition of immortals now fortifies Aeneas for the coming campaign: he receives help from the gods Tiberinus, Venus, and Vulcan. Tiberinus helps Aeneas by telling him how to find help from a mortal, King Evander. Evander's immediate recognition of Aeneas—Evander knew Anchises and notices the family resemblance—prompts him to offer his hand without hesitation to form a pact with Aeneas. This gesture of automatic trust and loyalty is founded both on Aeneas's reputation and on his family lineage, two elements of character that rank among the highest values of heroic culture. The Trojans obtain the reinforcements they need in large part because they are recognized and even expected—their coming has been heralded in prophecy far and wide. Everywhere they tread, the famous name of Troy earns them respect and hospitality.

The rich description of Aeneas's shield parallels Homer's description, in the *Iliad,* of the shield that Vulcan—known in the *Iliad* by his Greek name, Hephaestus—makes for Achilles. By emulating Homer, Virgil responds to and attempts to surpass the Greek tradition with the Roman. This desire to surpass was also evident in Augustan Rome, the Golden Age during which Virgil wrote, as the Roman Empire strove to outshine the accomplishments of ancient Greece. Aeneas's taking up of the new armor also symbolizes the way he symbolically shoulders the whole weight of the destiny of Rome.

Like Anchises' speech in Book VI, Virgil's description of the mural on the shield Vulcan forges for Aeneas promotes the Roman legend and stresses Augustus's position as the culmination of that legend. Repeating some of the scenes that Anchises describes in the underworld, Virgil particularly emphasizes the contrast between Romulus's humble beginnings and Caesar's far-reaching glory. As before, Virgil compresses the many centuries that separate Romulus from Augustus into a few lines, which heightens the impact of the contrast.

This rags-to-riches progression is a good tool for Virgil because it parallels the *Aeneid*'s plot: Aeneas and his followers leave Troy as refugees without a home, but go on to found a new and greater city in Italy. The city that the Trojans eventually establish—to be called Lavinium, after Lavinia—is not the site of Rome. Centuries later, Rome will be built by Romulus and Remus further up the Tiber, near where the Arcadians dwell when Aeneas approaches them to form an alliance. Aeneas's excursion away from the main scene of action brings him to the land that will become Rome. To Roman audiences, this powerful geographic connection would make more concrete their understanding of Aeneas as the founding father of their civilization.

BOOK IX

SUMMARY

Never one to miss an opportunity, Juno sends her messenger, Iris, down from Olympus to inform Turnus that Aeneas is away from his camp. With their leader gone, the Trojans are particularly vulnerable to an attack, so Turnus immediately leads his army toward the enemy camp. The Trojans spot the army coming and secure themselves inside their newly constructed fortress, unwilling to risk an open battle while Aeneas is away. Finding no obvious weakness in their defenses, Turnus decides to circumnavigate the camp and set fire to the defenseless ships anchored on the shore.

The fleet's destruction seems inevitable, but an old blessing prevents the ships' incineration. At the fleet's construction, Cybele—mother of the gods and sister of Saturn—requested her son Jupiter to render the vessels immortal because they were built of wood from trees in her sacred forest. As Turnus and his troops watch the ships burn, the vessels suddenly pull loose of their anchors, submerge, and reappear as sea nymphs. This sign vexes the Latins, but Turnus remains confident and determined to complete his annihilation of the Trojans, portents from the gods notwithstanding. Night falls, and the Latins make camp around the Trojan fortress.

The Trojans know that they must send reports of the Latins' movements to Aeneas quickly. Nisus and Euryalus, two friends eager for glory and adventure, volunteer to sneak out in the dark of night. The Trojan captains applaud the bravery of the two men. Quietly leaving the fortress, the two find the entire Latin army fast asleep. They pull their swords and begin slaughtering many great captains. When daylight approaches, they finally make their way toward the woods, but not before Euryalus takes the high helmet of a dead Latin captain as a prize. As they approach the forest, a group of enemy horsemen returning to camp through the woods sees the helmet flash in the distance, and rides toward the two Trojans. Nisus manages to escape into the woods, but the horsemen capture Euryalus. Nisus rushes back to save his friend, but in the end both are killed. The Latins put the heads of the two Trojans on stakes and parade them before the Trojan fortress, to the dismay of those inside.

Then the Latins attack. They cross the trenches surrounding the Trojan fortress and try to identify a weak spot in the walls, holding up their shields to block the barrage of spears that the Trojans hurl down from above. There is a high tower standing just outside the main gate, which Turnus lights on fire. Turnus and his men collapse the tower, killing many Trojans inside. The Trojans within the fortress begin to panic, but Ascanius renews their hope, getting his first taste of war when he fires an arrow through the head of Remulus, one of the Latin captains. Their confidence renewed, the Trojans open the gates and surprise the Latins by rushing out in attack, inflicting many Latin casualties in one quick strike. Unfortunately for the Trojans, Turnus joins the fray, suppresses the Trojans' surge, and begins to force them to retreat to the fortress. The Trojan Pandarus, observing the turning tide of battle, quickly shuts the gates again, allowing as many of his comrades as possible back inside—but letting Turnus through as well. Finally inside the enemy camp, the Latin leader kills Trojans as though it were an easy game. Eventually, though, Turnus is outnumbered, and narrowly escapes by jumping into the Tiber and floating back out to his comrades.

ANALYSIS

Throughout the poem, interventions on the part of the immortals tend to be spontaneous, responding to mortal affairs as they unfold. But Virgil's contention, while describing the burning Trojan fleet, that the fleet is immune to fire because of Cybele's blessing reads as a contrived act of retroactive *deus ex machina*. *Deus ex machina* literally means "god from the machine," and it is a device used to diffuse or solve a seemingly impossible situation by means of the spontaneous act of a divine hand. It is strange that we are not told about the immunity of the ships beforehand, given that we are told, for instance, that when the Trojans eat their own tables they will know they have arrived at their final destination.

Even stranger is the fact that the miraculous transformation of the Trojan ships into sea nymphs, though the result of a god's work, does not benefit the Trojans at all. Sea nymphs are not fit for sailing, so the Trojans lose their fleet despite divine intervention on their behalf. The Latins ultimately accomplish their mission of rendering the Trojan fleet useless, meaning that the Trojans are unable to flee the battle by sailing back out to sea. They are now grounded, and it is certain that the events of the epic are to be played out on Italian soil. Aesthetically, the transformation of the Trojan ships into sea nymphs is a sublime ending to the journey of a fleet of vessels that, from the epic's inception, has been buffeted by constant torments

and trials. To go down in flames while at anchor ashore would be a fate unworthy of ships that have endured such harshness at sea. Their underwater metamorphosis proves their status as heroic objects of war.

Virgil flirts with the defeat of the Trojans when, after Turnus gains access to the Trojan fortress, the author claims that if it had occurred to Turnus to open the gates and let his awaiting forces into the citadel, the Latins would have won the war then and there. By pointing to the possibility of other outcomes, Virgil heightens the dramatic import of the battle and establishes the Latins as worthy enemies. At the same time, this comment suggests that Turnus is not as amazing as he may seem, as it points out a shortcoming in his cunning and strategy.

In Book IX, Virgil foregrounds the parallels between the *Aeneid* and the *Iliad*. Turnus, for example, openly claims to be in the same predicament as the Greek king Menelaus—a Trojan has swept away Turnus's bride, Lavinia, just as the Trojan Paris made off with Menelaus's bride, Helen, thus bringing about the Trojan War. Turnus boasts that the Latins will not need to use the trickery of a wooden horse, as Odysseus did to gain entrance to Troy. Rather, he claims, the Latins will defeat the Trojans outright. Knowing the destined outcome of the war, we see that Turnus spells out his doom here: there may be similarities between the Greek-Trojan conflict and the Latin-Trojan conflict, but their outcomes will not be the same. The gods have offered clear signs that the conflict will turn in Aeneas's favor, but Turnus chooses to ignore them, denying any faith in the oracles of his demise. Turnus is a fearsome warrior who is either too assured of his own ability—a quality that, when combined with defiance of divine powers, is known as hubris—or is resigned to his role as a pure destructive obstacle to the Trojans. He hints at the latter sentiment when he cries, "I have my fate as well, to combat theirs" (IX.190).

The ill-fated journey of the eager young soldiers Nisus and Euryalus provides a poignant counterpoint to the Trojans' success at staving off the fortress's siege. Their youthful bravery is extinguished because of Euryalus's desire for prizes before the completion of their mission. They could easily kill a few Latins and still make it into the forest in good time. Instead, Euryalus concerns himself with the spoils of battle, enabling the Latins to capture him. Nisus's willingness to sacrifice his own life for his friend is noble but largely useless, as he does not manage to save Euryalus but does

SUMMARY & ANALYSIS

manage to stab Euryalus's killer as he falls to his own death. Following this intense and emotional episode, Virgil offers a brief message of memorial to these two Trojans, writing:

> Fortunate, both [Nisus and Euryalus]!
> If in the least my songs
> Avail, no future day will ever take you
> Out of the record of remembering Time.
> (IX.633–636)

In narrating the episode, Virgil displays his skill at dramatizing the impulsive, emotional nature of friendship and loyalty. With these lines to Nisus and Euryalus, he displays his confidence in his work and legacy, asserting that his poetry can make men immortal.

BOOK X

SUMMARY

From Olympus, Jupiter takes notice of the carnage in Italy. He had expected the Trojans to settle there peacefully, and he summons a council of all the gods to discuss the matter. There, Venus blames Juno for the continued suffering of Aeneas and the Trojans. Juno angrily responds that she did not force Aeneas to go to Italy. Annoyed at their bickering, Jupiter decrees that henceforth he will not help either side, so that the merits and efforts of men will decide their ends.

Meanwhile, the Latins continue their siege of the Trojan fortress, and Aeneas journeys back toward the battle. By this point, the army no longer has to march, because another king, Tarchon of Tuscany, has provided Aeneas with a fleet of ships, along with many great warriors to augment his forces. Sped on by the sea nymphs that were born of the Trojan fleet's transformation, the new fleet reaches the beach near the battlefield shortly after dawn. Turnus spots the ships approaching and leads his troops toward the beach to confront them. The Trojans disembark, and the battle commences.

Aeneas strikes the first blows, cutting down several of Turnus's men. The rest of the soldiers on both sides then fall into the fray, and blood begins to spill. Pallas leads the Arcadians, fighting fiercely and tipping the scales in favor of the Trojans. Already a great warrior in spite of his youth, he dispenses death with every blow, but attracts the attention of Turnus. Turnus swaggers forth and challenges Pallas alone in the center of the battle. They each toss their spears. Pallas's weapon penetrates Turnus's shield and armor, but leaves only a flesh wound on Turnus. Turnus's lance, on the other hand, tears through Pallas's corselet and lodges deep in his chest, killing him. Supremely arrogant after this kill, Turnus reaches down and rips off Pallas's belt as a prize.

Word of Pallas's death reaches Aeneas, who flies into a rage. He hacks a bloody path through the Latin lines, looking for Turnus and bent on vengeance. Terrified, some of the Latin soldiers beg on their knees to be spared, but Aeneas slaughters them mercilessly, and Turnus's troops fall into chaos. Up on Olympus, Juno sees that the battle is lost and asks Jupiter to let her spare Turnus from death. Jupiter consents, so Juno flies down to the battlefield, disguises herself as Aeneas, and comes within sight of Turnus. He chases her, and she runs onto one of the ships anchored nearby. Turnus follows, but as soon as he boards the ship, she severs the moorings and the ship floats out to sea. Powerless to return to the battlefield, Turnus drifts until the wind carries him ashore far down the coast.

In Turnus's absence, the great Latin warrior Mezentius takes up the fight. He slays many brave Trojans, but loses heart when Aeneas takes down his son, Lausus. He confronts the Trojan hero and casts a slew of spears at him, but the shield forged by Vulcan holds strong. In the end, Aeneas cuts down Mezentius as well, spelling defeat for the Latin army.

ANALYSIS

Jupiter's declaration that the rest of the battle will be waged entirely without divine interference comes as a surprise, as up to this point, humans have not had control over events. Though a divine hand does reach down once more before the battle's end when Juno persuades Jupiter to let her save Turnus, Jupiter grants Juno's request only because Venus herself is already protecting Aeneas. For the most part, the outcome of the battle is decided by the valor of the soldiers themselves.

Yet Jupiter's suspension of divine influence does not release the combatants from their fates. Jupiter's prohibition of interference only lends weight to the tragedy of the events that follow. By their own actions, which are determined by their own wills and abilities, the warriors bring their fates to pass as the conflict plays out.

Ironically, Turnus's killing of Pallas is the battle's turning point, as events then start to shift in the Trojans' favor. First, Virgil foreshadows the demise of the Latins when he says that by taking the belt of Pallas—an act of arrogance or hubris—Turnus spells his own doom. Pallas's death awakens in Aeneas a passion not witnessed since the fall of Troy—a mixture of ruthlessness, unrelenting anger, and hell-bent vengeance. The reappearance of Aeneas as a great warrior breaks the battle's stalemate.

Turnus's humiliation when Juno lures him away from the battle and onto the ship plays out to the further advantage of the Trojans. Turnus feels alienated from Juno, as though his advocate has suddenly become his adversary. She protects his person but not his honor, and impedes him in his single-minded commitment to behave as a heroic warrior whatever the cost. If the Trojans were to kill Turnus, their victory would be complete, but the fact that Turnus is involuntarily plucked from the battlefield by his immortal benefactor represents a moral victory for the Trojans. It boosts their spirits while deflating the Latins' pride.

Again in Book X, the Latins draw parallels between themselves and the Greeks who defeated the Trojans at Troy. This time, though, they invoke the Greeks as a contrast. The Greeks did not succeed in eliminating the Trojans altogether, as the Latins intend to do in Italy. The high irony is that the Latins are correct in saying that they are not like the Greeks—but primarily because they are not, in fact, capable of defeating the Trojans. Worse, the Greeks were able to defeat the Trojans on the Trojans' own ground; the Latins, on the other hand, prove incapable of defending their homeland. It is thus the Trojans, who can be viewed as invaders despite their invitation from King Latinus, who play the role of the Greeks, winning a war on enemy turf.

The difference between the Greeks in Troy and the Trojans in Italy lies in the Trojans' intention to settle in Italy and found what will become an empire. When the Greeks sacked Troy, they did so to reclaim a woman, and, with Helen retrieved, they set sail for home. Aeneas, on the other hand, must claim rather than reclaim a land, and he and the Trojans must justify their invasion of Italy by proclaiming the superiority of the race and culture that will result from the conquest.

Book XI

Summary

The day after the battle, Aeneas views the body of young Pallas and, weeping, arranges for 1,000 men to escort the prince's corpse to King Evander and to join the king in mourning. When Evander hears of his son's death, he is crushed, but because Pallas died honorably, he forgives Aeneas in his heart and wishes only for the death of Turnus.

Back at the battlefield, messengers arrive from the Latins, who request a twelve-day truce so that both sides may bury their dead. Aeneas agrees to the ceasefire. The messengers are impressed with Aeneas's piety. They think to themselves that Turnus should settle the quarrel over Lavinia in a duel with Aeneas to avoid further battle.

At a council called by King Latinus, others echo the messengers' sentiment. There, the Latins learn that Diomedes, the great Greek warrior who fought at Troy and now reigns over a nearby kingdom, has rejected their plea for aid. Latinus confesses that he does not think they can win, and proposes the offering of some territory to the Trojans in exchange for peace. A man named Drancës speaks, blaming the whole war on Turnus's arrogance. He claims that the rest of the Latins have lost the will to fight. The council begins to turn against Turnus, who, back from his foray on the ship, responds in anger. He challenges the courage and manhood of Drancës and Latinus, insulting the former and begging the latter to continue fighting. Still, Turnus says, if the council wishes him to fight Aeneas alone, he will do so without fear.

Just at that moment, a messenger arrives to warn the Latins that the Trojans are marching toward the city. Forgetting their debate, the Latins rush in a panic to prepare their defenses, joined now by Camilla, the famous leader of the Volscians, a race of warrior maidens. Turnus hears from a spy that Aeneas has divided his army: the light horses gallop toward the city while Aeneas and the heavily armored captains take a slower path through the mountains. Turnus rushes off to lay a trap for the Trojan leader on a particular mountain path, leaving the defense of the city to Camilla.

Soon the Trojans reach the field in front of the city, and the battle begins. Camilla proves the fiercest warrior present, scattering Aeneas's troops with her deadly spears and arrows. She brings down many soldiers before a Tuscan named Arruns catches her off guard, piercing her with his javelin. Unfortunately for him, the goddess Diana holds Camilla in high favor and dispatches her attendant Opis down from Olympus to kill Arruns as an act of revenge, cutting his personal victory short.

Having lost their leader in Camilla, the Latin troops scatter and flee back to the city. Many are killed in the retreat. Meanwhile, Camilla's companion Acca goes off to inform Turnus that the Latins lack a leader. Turnus is forced to return to the city just as Aeneas passes by the place of the ambush. Aeneas and Turnus return to their respective armies to make camp as night falls.

ANALYSIS

With the gods refraining from intervention in Aeneas's movements, Aeneas's words and actions reveal his integrity. His sincere mourning at Pallas's funeral shows how deeply he appreciates the youth's valor in arms and how seriously he took his promise to King Evander to protect the boy. Aeneas also honorably agrees to a truce so that the dead of both sides can be properly buried. His earlier descent to the underworld allows him to witness the terrible fate of those not properly buried on Earth—they roam the shores of the river Acheron, without a home and without rest. As a new aspect of his piety, Aeneas takes up the imperative that no one, not even his enemies in battle, should endure this awful punishment on his account.

But Aeneas has not conducted himself entirely as a paragon of mercy in the struggle with the Latins. In Book X, he mercilessly kills two Latins who are on their knees, begging him to spare their lives. In portraying Aeneas as a man who expresses many different emotional extremes—anger, hatred, passivity, grief, love, and pious respect—Virgil risks introducing some inconsistencies in his hero's character. Of course, it is certainly possible that a man could be both brutally unforgiving in war and lovingly compassionate at other times. However, our attempt to reconcile these two contradictory sides of Aeneas's heroism resembles Dido's failure to comprehend Aeneas's expression of love for her just before his act of abandonment. In both cases, Aeneas's primary motivations lie in fate and piety, but in the brief moments when fate and piety do not govern his actions, Aeneas expresses his true emotions either tenderly or brutally.

Turnus's character remains consistent, if somewhat one-dimensional. He is as stubborn and temperamental as ever. Drancës' claim that the war is Turnus's fault holds some truth, for King Latinus has opposed battle from the very beginning. Originally, Turnus claims to be fighting for his promised bride, Lavinia, but in the council it appears that his own pride has usurped Lavinia as his motivation. Both Latinus and Drancës insult Turnus by suggesting that he should be willing to lay down his arms in front of the Trojans after fighting for so long. Turnus's reply to the council is bitterly sarcastic, adding new depth to his character as he shows himself to be either ignorant or recklessly defiant. He seems hellbent on destruction, despite the warning signs of the gods in the earlier battles. He has too much at stake in terms of honor and reputation to give up now.

The action of Book XI suggests that the movement and success of the armies depend entirely upon visible and active leaders. The tide turns in battle when a leader either arrives on the scene or leaves it. When Camilla dies, for example, the Trojans scatter the Latins. Because the battles in the *Aeneid* always flow this way, it is necessary for Virgil, at times, to remove the greatest heroes from the fighting for a while in order to maintain some suspense—otherwise, Aeneas and Turnus would have met in single combat long ago. In Book XI, Turnus's planned ambush in the mountains removes the main characters from the fighting and then, coincidentally, keeps them from meeting at the last moment. Virgil delays this final confrontation for as long as possible, thus building the tension.

BOOK XII

SUMMARY

> *Just so Trojan Aeneas and the hero*
> *Son of Daunus, battering shield on shield,*
> *Fought with a din that filled the air of heaven.*
>
> (See QUOTATIONS, p. 64)

Turnus decides to go and fight Aeneas alone for both the kingdom and Lavinia's hand. King Latinus and Queen Amata protest, wanting Turnus to surrender and protect his life, but Turnus ignores their pleas, valuing his honor over his life. Latinus draws up the appropriate treaty, with Aeneas's consent. The next day, the armies gather as spectators on either side of a field in front of the city.

Juno worries about Turnus because she suspects that Aeneas outmatches him. She calls Juturna, Turnus's sister, and tells her to watch out for her brother's safety. Latinus and Aeneas both come out onto the battlefield, and each vows to uphold his side of the pact. But Juturna, not wanting her brother to risk the duel, appears to the Latin army disguised as a noble officer named Camers and goads the Latins to break the treaty and fight now that the Trojans are off their guard. Turnus's troops begin to agree, and suddenly one of them hurls a spear at the Trojans' ranks, killing a young soldier. This unprovoked shot ignites both armies. They fly at each other with sword and lance. Aeneas calls for his men to stop, but as he yells, a stray arrow wounds him in the leg, forcing him to retreat.

Watching Aeneas leave the field gives Turnus new hope. He enters the battle and lays waste to a slew of soldiers on the Trojan side. Meanwhile, Aeneas is helped back to camp, but the physician cannot remove the arrow from his leg. Venus pities her suffering son and sends down a healing balm. The physician uses the balm, dislodging the arrow and closing the wound.

Aeneas takes up his arms again and returns to the battle, where the Latin troops before him scatter in terror. Both he and Turnus kill many men, turning the tide of the battle back and forth. Suddenly, Aeneas realizes that Latinus's city has been left unguarded. He gathers a group of soldiers and attacks the city, panicking its citizens. Queen Amata, seeing the Trojans within the city walls, loses all hope and hangs herself. Turnus hears cries of suffering from the city and rushes back to the rescue. Not wanting his people to suffer further, he calls for the siege to end and for Aeneas to emerge and fight him hand-to-hand, as they had agreed that morning. Aeneas meets him in the city's main courtyard, and at last, with all the troops circled round, the duel begins.

First, Aeneas and Turnus toss their spears. They then exchange fierce blows with their swords. At Turnus's first strike, his sword suddenly breaks off at the hilt—in his haste, he had grabbed some other soldier's weaker sword. Turnus flees from Aeneas, calling for his real sword, which Juturna finally furnishes for him. Juno observes the action from above, and Jupiter asks her why she bothers—she already knows the struggle's inevitable outcome. Juno finally gives in and consents to abandon her grudge against Aeneas, on one condition: she wants the victorious Trojans to take on the name and the language of the Latins. Jupiter gladly agrees.

Jupiter sends down one of the Furies, who assumes the form of a bird and flaps and shrieks in front of Turnus, filling him with terror and weakening him. Seeing Turnus waver, Aeneas casts his mighty spear and strikes Turnus's leg, and Turnus tumbles to the ground. As Aeneas advances, Turnus pleads for mercy for the sake of his father. Aeneas is moved—but just as he decides to let Turnus live, he sees the belt of Pallas tied around Turnus's shoulder. As Aeneas remembers the slain youth, his rage returns in a surge. In the name of Pallas, Aeneas drives his sword into Turnus, killing him.

ANALYSIS

Since Turnus's entrance in Book VII, his behavior has been brash, confident, and self-assured, yet he shows himself to be vulnerable and complacent in this final book of the *Aeneid*. Even before his final battle with Aeneas, he seems to have surrendered to the fates he earlier resists. When he sees the city of Latinus awake with flame, he says to Juturna that fate has defeated his forces and that he has resigned himself to his death. The Turnus we hear uttering these words hardly seems the same man who, earlier in the epic, taunts the Trojans, insulting their manhood and calling them "twice-conquered" (IX.837) and "effete" (IX.860), or lacking vitality. When he begs Aeneas for mercy on his knees, ignoring the fact that he has lost in fair combat and thus deserves to die, he hardly seems the same man who earlier values his honor more than his life. Virgil provides little explanation for Turnus's transformation other than Turnus's dismay at hearing of the queen's suicide and the attack on the city. But, clearly, Virgil could not allow death to transform Turnus from Aeneas's mortal nemesis into a tragic hero. We might feel some sympathy for Turnus's resilience against the fates, but it represents the opposite of Aeneas's pious submission to the decrees of fate.

Juno undergoes a similar turnaround at the epic's conclusion. Until her conversation with Jupiter in Book XII, she stubbornly ignores the fates in her persecution of Aeneas. She knows she cannot win, but nevertheless she wants Aeneas to suffer, for her own satisfaction. Yet when Jupiter again points out that Aeneas is destined to prevail, as he has done often enough before, Juno suddenly crumbles, asking only that the Latin name and language be preserved. Like Turnus, Juno drives the plot of the *Aeneid* more than Aeneas does. Her sudden resignation represents the end of the epic's major conflict, as the antagonistic, tempestuous, and willful characters are subdued by the forces of order.

The poem ends with a somber description of Turnus's death: "And with a groan for that indignity [of death] / [Turnus's] spirit fled into the gloom below" (XII.1297–1298). Virgil does not narrate the epic's true resolution, the supposedly happy marriage between Aeneas and Lavinia and the initiation of the project of building Rome. Two elements of the classical tradition influence this ending. First, Virgil is again imitating Homer, whose *Iliad* concludes with the death of Hector, the great Trojan enemy of the Greek hero Achilles. Second, Virgil wants his Roman audience to feel that they themselves, not Aeneas's exploits, are the glorious conclusion to this epic story.

IMPORTANT QUOTATIONS EXPLAINED

1.   I sing of warfare and a man at war.
     From the sea-coast of Troy in early days
     He came to Italy by destiny,
     To our Lavinian western shore,
     A fugitive, this captain, buffeted
     . . .
     Till he could found a city and bring home
     His gods to Laetium, land of the Latin race,
     The Alban lords, and the high walls of Rome.
     Tell me the causes now, O Muse, how galled
     . . .
     From her old wound, the queen of gods compelled him—
     . . .
     To undergo so many perilous days
     And enter on so many trials. Can anger
     Black as this prey on the minds of heaven?

                                              (I.1–19)

With these opening lines of the *Aeneid,* Virgil enters the epic tradition in the shadow of Homer, author of the *Iliad,* an epic of the Trojan War, and the *Odyssey,* an epic of the Greek hero Ulysses' wanderings homeward from Troy. By naming his subjects as "warfare and a man," Virgil establishes himself as an heir to the themes of both Homeric epics. The man, Aeneas, spends the first half of the epic wandering in search of a new home and the second half at war fighting to establish this homeland. Lines 2 through 4 summarize Aeneas's first mission in the epic, to emigrate from Troy to Italy, as a fate already accomplished. We know from Virgil's use of the past tense that what he presents is history, that the end is certain, and that the epic will be an exercise in poetic description of historical events. In the phrase "our Lavinian . . . shore," Virgil connects his audience, his Roman contemporaries, to Aeneas, the hero of "early days."

Even though we do not learn Aeneas's name in these lines, we learn much about him. The fact that Aeneas's name is withheld for so long—until line 131—emphasizes Aeneas's lack of importance as an individual; his contribution to the future defines him. He is a "fugitive" and a "captain" and therefore a leader of men. That he bears responsibility to "bring home / His gods" introduces the concept of Aeneas's piety through his duty to the hearth gods of Troy. Most important, we learn that Aeneas is "a man apart, devoted to his mission." Aeneas's detachment from temporal and emotional concerns and his focus on the mission of founding Rome, to which Virgil alludes in the image of walls in line 12, increase as the epic progresses.

In this opening passage, Virgil mentions the divine obstacle that will plague Aeneas throughout his quest: the "sleepless rage" of the "queen of gods," Juno. Aeneas will suffer in the face of storms at sea and, later, a war on land, and Virgil attributes both these impediments to Juno's cruelty. In line 13, the poet asks the muse to explain the causes of Juno's ire. The invocation of a muse is the traditional opening line to an epic in the classical tradition beginning with Homer. Virgil delays his invocation of the muse by a dozen lines, first summarizing what might be considered a matter of mortal history, and then inquiring the muse of the matter's divine causes.

Virgil's question, "Can anger / Black as this prey on the minds of heaven?" brings up the ancients' relationship to the gods. Within their polytheistic religious system, the Greeks and Romans reckoned the will of the gods to be the cause of all events on Earth. Instead of attributing forces of good and evil to the gods, as later religions did, the Greeks and Romans believed the gods to be motivated by emotions recognizable to humans—jealousy, vanity, pride, generosity, and loyalty, for example. The primary conflict in the *Aeneid* is Juno's vindictive anger against the forces of fate, which have ordained Aeneas's mission to bring Troy to Italy, enabling the foundation of Rome.

2.   Did you suppose, my father,
      That I could tear myself away and leave you?
      Unthinkable; how could a father say it?
      Now if it pleases the powers about that nothing
      Stand of this great city; if your heart
      Is set on adding your own death and ours
      To that of Troy, the door's wide open for it.

                                        (II.857–863)

In this passage from Book II, which precedes Aeneas's flight from burning Troy with his father upon his back, Virgil distinguishes Aeneas for his piety. This sense of duty has two components. The first is a filial component: Aeneas is a dutiful son to Anchises, and he wants to escape with him to safety. Aeneas makes it plain that his strong sense of family loyalty will not allow him to abandon Anchises. The second is a social component: Anchises, Aeneas argues, cannot choose to stay and die at Troy without affecting many others. Anchises is a patriarch, and were he to resign himself to death, he would effectively choose death for them all. These words of Aeneas's lift Anchises out of the self-indulgence of despair and remind him of the leadership role that his seniority and status demand. In the ensuing episodes, even after his death, Anchises serves as a wise counselor to his son as Aeneas makes his way toward Italy.

QUOTATIONS

3. Roman, remember by your strength to rule
    Earth's peoples—for your arts are to be these:
    To pacify, to impose the rule of law,
    To spare the conquered, battle down the proud.
    (VI.1151–1154)

This passage is part of the speech Anchises delivers to Aeneas in the underworld, in Book VI, as he unfolds for his son the destiny of Rome. Virgil places his own political ideals in the mouth of the wise father, warning that the Roman nation should be more merciful than violent, even in its conquests. Virgil here propounds the values for which he wants Rome to stand, and which he believes he has, in his own time, let guide him. Anchises' rhetoric here about the Roman Empire's justification for its conquering of other peoples expresses the same justification that Aeneas and the Trojans make for settling in Rome. They defend their invasion by arguing that they bring justice, law, and warfare—with which they "pacify" and "battle down"—to the conquered. Especially in modern times, critics and readers have taken passages such as this one and labeled them propaganda for the Augustan regime. This criticism is valid, but when the values of a regime are expressed by a poet who shares those values, the line between art and propaganda becomes blurry.

4.   Amata tossed and turned with womanly
      Anxiety and anger. Now [Allecto]
      Plucked one of the snakes, her gloomy tresses,
      And tossed it at the woman, sent it down
      Her bosom to her midriff and her heart,
      . . .
      Slipping between her gown and her smooth breasts
      . . .
      While the infection first, like dew of poison
      Fallen on her, pervaded all her senses,
      Netting her bones in fire.

                                    (VII. 474–490)

This vivid and disturbing description of the means by which the Fury Allecto incites Amata's rage against Aeneas occurs in Book VII. Virgil plays on our senses, using images of fire, disease, poison, and sex to describe the passionate anger Amata feels at seeing her daughter's proposed marriage thwarted and at hearing that a Trojan exile is to become part of her household. Virgil expresses the idea of being hot with anger by employing the images of things that, literally or figuratively, can heat a human's blood. The invisible snake deployed by Allecto acts to enhance emotions already latent within Amata, since Amata already feels "womanly / Anxiety and anger" of her own. Even though Amata has perfectly good reason to despise Aeneas and the Trojans, Virgil explains her hatred by placing it physically in her body, suggesting that she incites war in the way she does because there is something wrong inside her. The snake unleashed by Juno essentially has a sexual encounter with Amata—it is as though Juno has impregnated Amata with madness.

QUOTATIONS

5. When two bulls lower heads and horns and charge
    In deadly combat . . .
        . . .
    [They g]ore one another, bathing necks and humps
    In sheets of blood, and the whole woodland bellows.
    Just so Trojan Aeneas and the hero
    Son of Daunus, battering shield on shield,
    Fought with a din that filled the air of heaven.

                                          (XII.972–982)

This passage from Book XII, in which Virgil describes Aeneas and
Turnus locked together in the heat of battle, exemplifies a literary
device Virgil employs throughout the poem: the epic simile. Virgil's
similes are extended comparisons of an element of action or a
character to an abstract or external image or concept. These similes are often drawn from rural landscapes and farm life, and they
often use the phrase "just so" as a connector. They give Virgil's
writing a descriptive richness by lingering at great length on some
detail that might not otherwise have been illuminated. Often, Virgil uses the similes to give an interior depth to his characters,
showing us by means of an analogy what it feels like to be that
character in a given moment. This particular epic simile describes
the intense battle between Aeneas and Turnus. By comparing these
two warriors to bulls, Virgil conveys the potent, animalistic nature
of their struggle.

KEY FACTS

FULL TITLE
  The *Aeneid*

AUTHOR
  Virgil

TYPE OF WORK
  Epic poem

GENRE
  Heroic epic; mythological story

LANGUAGE
  Latin

TIME AND PLACE WRITTEN
  Around 20 B.C., probably in Rome and in the north of Italy, and
  perhaps in Greece

DATE OF FIRST PUBLICATION
  Virgil died in 19 B.C., before he finished revising the *Aeneid*; it
  was published after his death.

NARRATOR
  The poet Virgil, although Aeneas himself assumes the narration
  in Books II and III, when he gives a retrospective account of his
  adventures

POINT OF VIEW
  When Virgil controls the narration, the point of view includes
  the actions of the gods as well as the human story; Aeneas, in his
  storytelling, does not have this access to the gods' perspective
  and relates events only from his own perspective.

TONE
  When treating the glory of Rome, the epic is solemn and
  honorific. When Virgil depicts the victims of history—those
  who suffered in the course of the founding of Rome, like Dido—
  his tone is tragic and sympathetic.

TENSE

Usually past, sometimes switching to present to increase the immediacy of a scene. Virgil also uses the future tense, for prophecy and prediction.

SETTING (TIME)

In the aftermath of the Trojan War, about 1000 B.C.

SETTING (PLACE)

The Mediterranean, including the north coast of Asia Minor, Carthage, and Italy

PROTAGONIST

Aeneas

MAJOR CONFLICT

Aeneas is fated to travel from the ruins of Troy to Italy, where he will establish a race that will lead to the founding of Rome. Juno, harboring feelings of vengeance against the Trojans, impedes Aeneas's mission by inciting a romance between Aeneas and Dido and then a war between the Trojans and the Latins, causing suffering for the hero, his fleet, and many whom they encounter on the way.

RISING ACTION

The epic has two parts: Aeneas's wanderings in Books I–VI, and his struggle to establish himself in Latium in Books VII–XII. In the first half of the epic, Aeneas tells the story of the siege of Troy and his escape, causing Dido to love him. In the second half of the epic, King Latinus offers the hand of his daughter, Lavinia, to Aeneas in marriage, and Juno responds by inciting rage in the hearts of Queen Amata and Turnus and then opening the Gates of War.

CLIMAX

In the first half of the epic, Venus and Juno contrive to isolate Dido and Aeneas in a cave during a hunting trip, and there the two lovers consummate their affair. In the second half of the epic, Turnus kills Pallas, inciting the lethal vengeance of Aeneas.

FALLING ACTION

In the first half of the epic, Aeneas leaves Carthage for Italy at Mercury's prodding, causing the heartbroken Dido to kill herself. In the second half, the war between the Trojans and the Latins comes down to a duel between Aeneas and Turnus.

Aeneas wins, and, after considering sparing his enemy's life, he decides to kill Turnus to avenge Pallas's death.

THEMES

The primacy of fate; the suffering of wanderers; the glory of Rome

MOTIFS

Prophecies and predictions; founding a new city; vengeance

SYMBOLS

Flames; the golden bough; the Gates of War; the Trojan hearth gods; weather

FORESHADOWING

The events of the epic narrative are already history to the Roman audience. The many dreams and prophecies of various characters reveal a veiled future to mortals and are the epic's strongest form of foreshadowing. Also, when Turnus kills Pallas, Virgil foreshadows Turnus's own death.

KEY FACTS

STUDY QUESTIONS & ESSAY TOPICS

STUDY QUESTIONS

1. *How negatively does Aeneas's abandonment of Dido reflect on his character?*

Though Aeneas cannot resist the will of the gods or fate, which demands that he leave Carthage, the manner in which he leaves Dido is not beyond contempt. We know from other passages that Aeneas is not a character without compassion, yet if Aeneas feels genuine sympathy for the lover he is about to abandon, he fails to express it well. He speaks formally and tersely to Dido, offers her little comfort, and denies that an official marriage bound them to each other. He refers to Troy and the new home he plans to found in Italy and talks of his son's future. We can find fault in Aeneas because, while Virgil allows us a view of Aeneas's emotions of sadness, regret, and reluctance as he leaves Carthage, Aeneas expresses little of these emotions to Dido. If we consider one's self to reside in one's will and emotions, Aeneas betrays himself by leaving Dido, and he admits as much, claiming that her words set them "both afire" (IV.498).

Both Aeneas and Dido face a conflict between civic responsibility and individual desire. Aeneas sides with his obligations, while Dido submits to her desires, and so their love is tragically impossible. In terms of his patriotic duty, Aeneas acts impeccably, though he may be faulted for staying with Dido in Carthage as long as he does. His abandonment of Dido is necessary his service to Troy, his allies, his son, his father, and fate. From this point of view, Aeneas acts correctly in subjecting his desires to the benefit of the Trojan people.

Dido fails her city by ignoring her civic duty from the point when she falls in love with Aeneas to her suicide. Virgil suggests that Dido's suicide mythically anticipates Rome's defeat of Carthage, hundreds of years later. How negatively we judge Aeneas for his abandonment of Dido depends not on whether we sympathize with or blame Dido, but on whether we believe that Aeneas's manner of leaving her—and not his departure itself—is what causes her suicide.

2.　*To what extent is the Aeneid a political poem? Is it propaganda?*

The *Aeneid*'s main purpose is to create a myth of origins that consolidates Rome's historical and cultural identity. This search for origins of a race or culture is a political endeavor, in that it seeks to justify the Roman Empire's existence and to glorify the empire through the poem's greatness. Yet the *Aeneid* is also an artistic endeavor, and therefore to dismiss the poem as mere propaganda is to ignore its obvious artistic merit.

In many of the passages referring explicitly to the emperor Augustus—in Anchises' presentation of the future of Rome, for example—Virgil's language suggests an honest and heartfelt appreciation of Augustus's greatness. It is worth noting, however, that in addition to being the emperor, Augustus was also Virgil's patron. It would thus have been impossible for Virgil to criticize him outright in his work. One can argue that Virgil may not have truly believed in Augustus's greatness and that the impossibility of explicit criticism forced him to resort to subtle irony in order to air any grievances regarding Augustus's policies or ideology.

3. *What is the relationship in the Aeneid between an individual's merit and the degree to which his or her personality is interesting? How might our estimation differ from Virgil's?*

In some ways, Juno, Dido, and Turnus are more developed, well-defined characters than Aeneas is. They act on their desires and emotions and assert their wills, and Virgil puts much of his best poetry into the words and descriptions of these three. Yet throughout the *Aeneid,* there is a straightforward appreciation of the order, duty, and piety embodied by Aeneas. He follows the will of the gods and respects the deceased and the unborn at the expense of his own happiness. Again and again, we are told that Aeneas suffers inwardly, despite his outward appearance. These qualities, though admirable, still do not make Aeneas the most vivid or captivating of heroes. They are important because they are the vaunted qualities Aeneas shares with Rome under the peaceful rule of Augustus.

SUGGESTED ESSAY TOPICS

1.   What is the role of dreams in the *Aeneid*?

2.   How do you explain the surprise alterations of character and abrupt ending of Book XII? How does Book XII fit in with the rest of the *Aeneid,* with respect to both characters and plot?

3.   Is the plot of the *Aeneid* driven more by the gods or by human characters? Does Aeneas, by himself, have the will to make it to Italy, or is it necessary for him to be prodded along the way?

4.   Why do you think Virgil starts the story in the middle and then spends two chapters on Aeneas's retrospective? What does he achieve with such a structure?

5.   How do Aeneas's piety and sense of duty change as the poem unfolds?

6.   How does the behavior of the gods reflect on human qualities?

7.   How are the various Italian peoples (Latins, Arcadians, Volscians) depicted, in relation to the Trojans and to each other?

REVIEW & RESOURCES

QUIZ

1. Which of the gods is the staunchest enemy of Aeneas and the Trojans?

   A. Jupiter
   B. Venus
   C. Neptune
   D. Juno

2. Who is the queen of Carthage, the city-state where Aeneas lands after the big storm in Book I?

   A. Venus
   B. Dido
   C. Cassandra
   D. Helen

3. What was hidden inside the wooden belly of the horse left outside the Trojan gates?

   A. Greek warriors
   B. Treasure
   C. Trojan hearth gods
   D. A bomb

4. Who does not die in the sack of Troy?

   A. King Priam
   B. Priam's son, Polites
   C. Aeneas's wife, Creusa
   D. Aeneas's son, Ascanius

5. What prophesy does the Harpy issue?

   A. That the Trojans will never make it to Italy
   B. That the Trojans will eat their own tables
   C. That Dido will commit suicide
   D. That Virgil will become the greatest Roman poet

6. Where does Anchises, Aeneas's father, die?

   A. Antander, near Troy
   B. Crete
   C. Italy
   D. Drepanum, in Sicily

7. Who breaks off the love affair between Aeneas and Dido?

   A. Aeneas
   B. Dido
   C. Dido's husband, Sychaeus
   D. Anchises

8. Where does Aeneas last see Dido?

   A. In Troy
   B. In Carthage
   C. In Rome
   D. In the underworld

9. How do the young Trojan boys participate in the contests in Sicily?

   A. They play an ancient Mediterranean form of lacrosse
   B. They have a wheelbarrow race
   C. They exhibit their horsemanship in a mock battle
   D. They are offered as prizes

10. Who sets fire to the Trojan fleet in Sicily, the first time the ships burn?

    A. Jupiter
    B. Juno
    C. Aeneas
    D. The women of Troy

11. What token must Aeneas carry to be admitted alive into the underworld?

   A.   A golden bough
   B.   A letter from his father
   C.   A lock of Dido's hair
   D.   The Sibyl

12. When Aeneas lands in Latium, how does he know he has come to the right place?

   A.   The ghost of his father appears
   B.   An emissary comes to meet him
   C.   The Trojans fulfill the Harpy's prediction by eating their "tables" of bread
   D.   He has a vision of the future glory of Rome

13. Who does not oppose the marriage of Lavinia to Aeneas?

   A.   Turnus
   B.   Latinus
   C.   Amata
   D.   Juno

14. What symbolizes the beginning of battle for the Latins?

   A.   A sacrifice to Mars
   B.   The donning of ritual armor
   C.   A procession in honor of ancient war heroes
   D.   The opening of the Gates of War

15. How does Evander know Aeneas's father, Anchises?

   A.   Anchises visited Arcadia when Evander was young
   B.   Evander grew up in Troy
   C.   They met in Carthage when both were guests of Dido
   D.   Anchises grew up in Arcadia

16. Who makes the strong and beautiful new armor Aeneas wears into battle?

    A. Jupiter
    B. Hercules
    C. Vulcan
    D. Cupid

17. Why do the Trojan ships turn into sea nymphs when Turnus tries to burn them?

    A. Because Venus intervenes
    B. Because the nymphs had been trapped in the hulls for a hundred years waiting to be released
    C. Because Ascanius's prayer is answered
    D. Because they were built out of wood sacred to Cybele

18. Who begs to be executed in place of his friend Euryalus?

    A. Turnus
    B. Nisus
    C. Pallas
    D. Ascanius

19. Who kills Pallas?

    A. Aeneas
    B. Turnus
    C. Dido
    D. Pygmalion

20. How does Juno get Turnus away from battle and onto a ship?

    A. She leaves a trail of bread crumbs
    B. She sends Iris to tell him the ship is burning
    C. She disguises herself as Aeneas and runs onto the ship
    D. She initiates a battle at sea

21. How long is the burial truce to which the two armies agree?

   A. 12 days
   B. 24 days
   C. 12 hours
   D. 24 hours

22. Which woman slays many Trojans in battle?

   A. Lavinia
   B. Amata
   C. Elissa
   D. Camilla

23. Who, besides Dido, commits suicide?

   A. Amata
   B. Turnus
   C. Hector
   D. Juno

24. What request does Juno make as she finally gives in to Aeneas's fated victory?

   A. That he have no descendents
   B. That Turnus be spared
   C. That Rome and Carthage be enemies for all time
   D. That Italy inherit the Latins' name and language and not the Trojans'

25. What counteracts Aeneas's impulse to spare Turnus's life?

   A. He knows Turnus will be ashamed to receive his mercy
   B. He sees the belt that Turnus took from the dead Pallas
   C. He remembers his father's warning
   D. He wants to avenge Dido's death

ANSWER KEY:
1: D; 2: B; 3: A; 4: D; 5: B; 6: D; 7: A; 8: D; 9: C; 10: D; 11: A; 12: C; 13: B; 14: D; 15: A; 16: C; 17: D; 18: B; 19: B; 20: C; 21: A; 22: D; 23: A; 24: D; 25: B

SUGGESTIONS FOR FURTHER READING

CAIRNS, FRANCIS. *Virgil's Augustan Epic.* New York: Cambridge University Press, 1989.

CAMPS, W. A. *An Introduction to Virgil's AENEID.* New York: Oxford University Press, 1969.

COMMAGER, STEELE, ed. *Virgil: A Collection of Critical Essays.* Englewood Cliffs, New Jersey: Prentice Hall, 1966.

FRANK, TENNEY. *Vergil, A Biography.* Oxford: Clarendon Press, 1922.

NITCHIE, ELIZABETH. *Vergil and the English Poets.* New York: Columbia University Press, 1919.

PUTNAM, MICHAEL. *The Poetry of the AENEID.* Cambridge: Harvard University Press, 1965.

QUINN, KENNETH. *Virgil's AENEID: A Critical Description.* London: Routledge and Kegan Paul, 1968.

SLAVITT, DAVID R. *Virgil.* New Haven: Yale University Press, 1991.

REVIEW & RESOURCES

A Note on the Type

The typeface used in SparkNotes study guides is Sabon, created by master typographer Jan Tschichold in 1964. Tschichold revolutionized the field of graphic design twice: first with his use of asymmetrical layouts and sanserif type in the 1930s when he was affiliated with the Bauhaus, then by abandoning assymetry and calling for a return to the classic ideals of design. Sabon, his only extant typeface, is emblematic of his latter program: Tschichold's design is a recreation of the types made by Claude Garamond, the great French typographer of the Renaissance, and his contemporary Robert Granjon. Fittingly, it is named for Garamond's apprentice, Jacques Sabon.

SparkNotes
Test Preparation
Guides

The SparkNotes team figured it was time to cut standardized tests down to size. We've studied the tests for you, so that SparkNotes test prep guides are:

Smarter:
Packed with critical-thinking skills and test-
taking strategies that will improve your score.

Better:
Fully up to date, covering all new features of the tests,
with study tips on every type of question.

Faster:
Our books cover exactly what you need to
know for the test. No more, no less.

SparkNotes Guide to the SAT & PSAT
SparkNotes Guide to the SAT & PSAT — Deluxe Internet Edition
SparkNotes Guide to the ACT
SparkNotes Guide to the ACT — Deluxe Internet Edition
SparkNotes Guide to the SAT II Writing
SparkNotes Guide to the SAT II U.S. History
SparkNotes Guide to the SAT II Math Ic
SparkNotes Guide to the SAT II Math IIc
SparkNotes Guide to the SAT II Biology
SparkNotes Guide to the SAT II Physics

SparkNotes Study Guides: